New Hotel Designs

New Hotel Designs

Olivier de Vleeschouwer

THE ART OF THE HABITAT

Series edited by Olivier Boissière

Front cover
Pfaulms Posthotel,
Pegnitz, Germany.
Designer: Dirk Obliers.

Back cover
Mondrian, Los Angeles,
United States.
Designer:
Philippe Starck.

Preceding page
Pousada de Nossa
Senhora da Asunção,
Arraiolos, Portugal.
Architect:
José Paulo dos Santos.

Editorial Director: Jean-François Gonthier
Art Director: Bruno Leprince
Cover design: Daniel Guerrier
Writers: Olivier de Vleeschouwer with Véronique Donnat and Olivier Boissière
English adaptation: Rubye Monet
Editing: Françoise Derray
Assistant: Sophie-Charlotte Legendre
Composition: Graffic, Paris
Filmsetting: Compo Rive Gauche, Paris
Lithography: Litho Service, T. Zamboni, Verona

ISBN : 2-7450-0031-4
Printed in the European Community

TELLERI - 30, rue de Charonne - F-75011 Paris

Contents

Introduction

In the past two decades there has grown up in the margins of the hotel trade a new type of establishment. These are hotels with a difference: they are colorful, expressive, more personalized than the run-of-the-mill luxury hotel. They play on the startling and the spectacular. The clientele they attract are young and wealthy, peripatetic city-dwellers, extroverts who enjoy the limelight, show business stars, would-be stars and groupies.

The new hotel genre is not without precedents: the architect Morris Lapidus was already working in this direction in Miami in the 1940s; John Portman created something of this type in the 1970s, but it was soon crushed by the norms and specifications, and the prevalent conformism of the hotel industry. Each in his own way and in the spirit of his time had created hotels of atmosphere (just as there were movie theaters built with a specific theme or atmosphere) where the guest found himself plunged into a decor of dream or fantasy, like an actor set down in the middle of an extravagant stage set. This idea of giving an air of theatricality to a semi-public place laid the foundations for theme hotels, of the type later championed by Disney.

Hotel im Wasserturm,
Cologne, Germany.
Designer:
Andrée Putman.

But the hotels that interest us here have nothing to do with theme parks or children's games. First of all, they were not, as is quite obvious, designed for children. The places invented by the developer Ian Schrager and his long-time accomplice Philippe Stark play on another register entirely: the call of pleasure or desire, the enjoyment of the allusive and the tongue-in-cheek, the wish to see and be seen. In other cases the theme has been chosen with a particular clientele in mind: the art world, for example, with its artists, dealers and art lovers; or that of music, the fans as well as the musicians; or the milieu of show business or advertising, myriad mini-societies of globetrotting pros or amateurs, who find in these out-of-the-ordinary surroundings the echos of their private cosmologies.

Far from the beaten track of mass tourism, these exclusive, sometimes elitist, always off-beat establishments proudly display the marks of their eclectic culture, creations of the foremost architects and designers of our time.

Andrée Putman

Morgans

New York, United States

A hotel that would be more like a house than a hotel, yet with all the facilities that fine hostelry demands. With this apparently simple idea, Ian Schrager created his concept of "Boutique Hotel" which, from Morgans to the Royalton, from the Paramount to the Delano, has impressed upon travelers' minds a new type of establishment, different from the traditional concept of a hotel as just a place to sleep. Reflecting the personality of its owner, this new kind of hotel offers a quality of services of a particular kind, more informal yet more attentive than we are accustomed to in an establishment of this category.

Ian Schrager and Steve Rubell chose Andrée Putman to redesign the interior for the first time in 1983. With her inimitable sense of "simple chic," the priestess of international design had a field day transforming the old building dating from 1929 into a temple of good taste, leaving no detail to chance. In 1995, when it seemed time to renew the interior design, Putman came in again, to work wonders with her light, sure touches and her infallible sense of color. Taupe, camel and ivory – with this range of tranquil elegance the designer offered Morgans a rejuvenation cure without a false note.

Behind its neo-classic limestone facade, Morgans has a

The neo-classical facade of Morgans on Madison Avenue in midtown Manhattan. Built in 1929, it has fought ever since, despite its size (154 rooms) and despite the ever-encroaching skyscrapers around it, to keep its calm and homelike warmth. All these qualities have been restored by Andrée Putman for the second time since 1983.

The lobby: a mix of styles from the first half of the century.

The restaurant Asia de Cuba designed by Philippe Starck.

Opposite page
In the lounge Putman plays with assorted chairs and profusion of candles (their number doubled by mirrored reflections). The total effect is not unlike a fireside nook you'd expect to find in a private home.

cozy hall, like a vast lounge that sets the tone for the rest. A hotel that doesn't look like a hotel. On the floor of Italian granite with chocolate-colored trompe-l'œil effects, club chairs and assorted armchairs exude comfort and an invitation to repose. The colors blend perfectly with the taupe-colored walls, lit here and there by discreet spotlights. In the evening, 1920s lamps and candles give the hall all the charm of a great family home.

For the design of the bar, Putman took her inspiration from the world of Jean Cocteau, a perfect blend of modernity with baroque references. The intentionally incongruous confrontation of disparate elements creates an impression as original as it is harmonious. Objects unearthed in New York flea markets, gilded sofas from the 18th-century and contemporary armchairs share the space on either side of an 8-meter long bar.

Since 1997, the restaurant Asia de Cuba, entirely conceived by Philippe Starck, offers Latino-Chinese food, a perfect combination of yang and yin. The restaurant is bathed in dim blue light and rings with the lilting rhythms of the samba. Just the sort of place that Schrager and Starck love, with an atmosphere conducive to easy encounters.

The 154 guest bedrooms repeat the same hushed tones of gray, ivory and taupe. The furniture is also part of the search for well-being and intimacy. Chairs covered in suede, silk or corduroy give a homey feeling so dear to Schrager. The window frames and the doors are of maple, wood being a material particularly prized by Andrée Putman. Black and white photos by Robert Mapplethorpe adorn the walls. The bathrooms recall the turn-of-the-century style of the Viennese Secession. Small black and white checks are multiplied in the Eileen Gray mirrors. On either side of the bathtub are washbasins like those used on planes. The lighting in the rooms is carefully planned to accentuate he feeling of gentle intimacy. The fact that there are only 4 to 8 rooms per floor add to the impression of harmony that so enthralls the visitor.

Andrée Putman has designed this space as if it were a private home. Hotel logistics are never allowed to interfere with the prevailing quiet. Not surprising in these conditions that Morgans defines itself as "the handsomest hotel in New York." □

In the bathroom, checkerboard squares and fittings by Ecart.

The billiard room, as dramatic as any theater set.

Opposite page
Two versions of the interior scenography: in both, the accent is on repose, reading or quiet conversation. Above, a cozy club chair with its footstool. Below, a window seat.

Each room is individualized, but in each the organization of space and furniture is built around a duality of sleep and waking activities, reading, writing, conversation.

It all seems so simple when Andrée Putman does it, but for such discreet elegance, every detail counts: the ample bed, the pure lines of the furniture, the window seat that is here a real sofa and the restful tones of cream and gray.

H
O
T
E
L
SORAT.
29

Johanne and Gernot Nalbach

Sorat Art'otel

Berlin, Germany

The bar, put together with humor and some nice touches of color – brick red for the counter, zigzag motif for the stools and a little ceiling of wavy metal.

Opposite page
On the Joachimstalerstrasse, a stone's throw from the famous Kurfürstndamm, the figure of a discus thrower looks down from the roof over the modest facade of the Sorat Art'Hotel. A classic figure for a not very classic hotel – for the artwork here is all resolutely contemporary.

The Sorat Art'otel, created in 1990, is the work of a husband-and-wife team of Viennese architects, Gernot and Johanne Nalbach. The result immediately attracted the attention of the public, not only for the design of the hotel but also for the large place given over to the work of the Berlin painter and sculptor Wolf Vostell, an artist of "fluxus and happening."

The design is a genuine coproduction, marked by such deep and total osmosis between the architects that it is difficult to separate who did what. Basically, Gernot took charge of the general design and structural organization of the hotel while the interior design was planned and carried out by his wife Johanne.

The original hotel, situated in the heart of West Berlin, consisted of 75 rooms. The idea was for each room to blend the practical and the poetic. At the same time, without ever abandoning a modernist approach, the Nalbachs have

Johanne Nalbach, who designed all the furniture, skillfully sets the stage in every area of the hotel, and throws in some surprising effects. Above: at the bar, a large cactus rears its prickly head.

Opposite page

Another eye-catcher in a corridor – an unusual structure offers guests the news of the day and, at the same time, is a geometry lesson based on circles, scrolls and ridges, around the central cone. Even the doors add some unexpected curves to the ensemble.

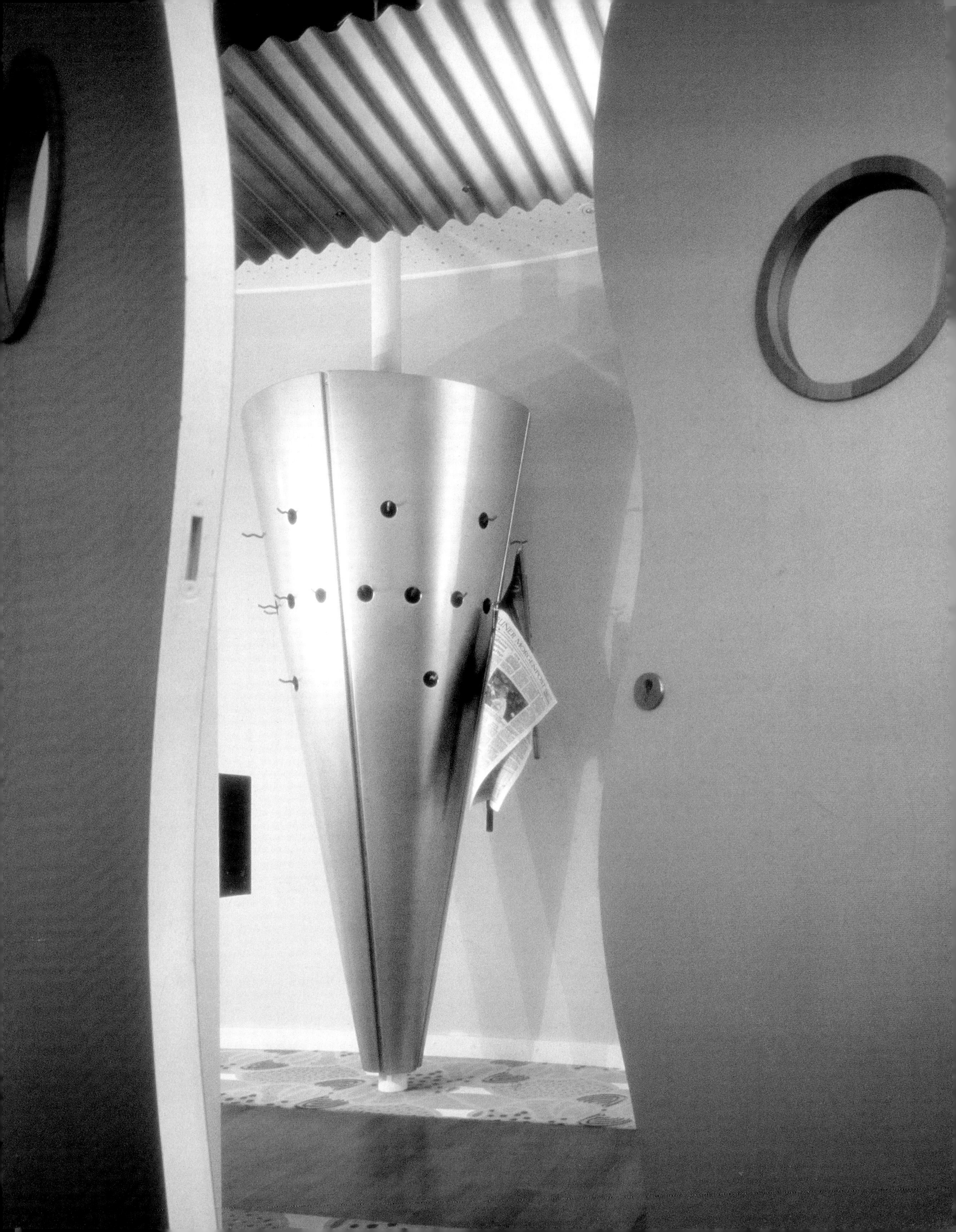

A sensual and feminine touch in the dining room. Broad-backed, no-nonsense chairs on carpeting with a graceful pattern of curves and spots. The same carpeting is present in all the public areas.

On the doors, an interesting textured pattern that makes one want to touch the relief. Here, too, undulating movement returns, looking rather like a wave, or perhaps a female reclining form.

always given a big role to nature, through their choice of materials and of forms utilized. The rippling waves of the Danube are suggested by the patterns on the walls and also in the line of the coverings that mask some of the electrical circuits. All the furniture was designed by Johanne in such a way as to be bright, functional and uncluttered. Color is a major component in the work of both these architects. They use it to add life and give a dynamic dimension to the space. For example, in the new wing, added in 1996 (with 56 additional rooms) they have matched the hallway carpet to the dominant color of each bedroom, creating an easily recognizable path to lead the guest to his room. Thus, it acts as a connecting thread between the outer and inner space and a dynamic link between what is already familiar and the still unknown space soon to be discovered inside the room. In the same way, a three-color harmony unites bedroom furnishings and the tiling of the bathroom. This desire to mark the imagination by intense colors, bright reds, deep blues and greens, contributes a lot to the distinctive identity of this very singular hotel.

Despite a certain classicism, the hotel has a multitude of details full of invention, poetry and humor. In the guest bedrooms, Johanne Nalbach has invented a masculine/feminine dialogue by choosing distinctive headboards for the beds: the man's side is generally darker, the woman's lighter. A round, light-colored cushion adorns the maple panel on the woman's side, while the man's cushion is square and practically black. Even the armchairs, through cleverly conceived details, make allusions to the male and female element.

In the bathrooms, the overall sobriety does not preclude some nice original touches. The conical washbasins are of polished steel and seem to float on square mirrors. As for the toilets themselves, the Nalbachs have followed the famous "bucket" model designed by Philippe Stark.

The Sorat has prominently featured the works of Wolf Vostell in every part of the building, but in the future, other artists will be more and more represented. The idea, here again, is to use the hotel (a place of passage par excellence) as a privileged space to arouse curiosity and enthusiasm. For a good many architects who have participated in the great hotel adventure during the past ten years, the common denominator seems to be expressed in a desire to provoke "action and reaction." □

The furniture borrows freely from assorted periods, which Johanne Nalbach puts together with grace and skill. Here, a spare, somewhat formal effect, with a chair and table inspired by the style of the fifties.

22 Sorat Art'otel, Berlin, Germany

One double bed with two distinctive sides – the broad maple headboard has an oval on the woman's side and a square on the man's. The overall effect is tongue-in-cheek and guests may transgress the signals with no risk whatsoever. An original lithograph by Wolf Vostell looks down on the scene.

Opposite page
A soft color scheme of pale gray, blue and green gives a feeling of great refinement. Another of the Wolf Vostell lithographs that are displayed at the Sorat. Here the furniture has a vague resemblance to the work of Philippe Starck. In the bathroom, a genuine Philippe Starck – the designer's famous "bucket" toilet.

明治生命
清酒
忠勇
フジシン
三洋信販

Aldo Rossi and Shigeru Uchida

Il Palazzo

Fukuoka, Japan

"Il grande cantiere di Fukuoka," as imagined by the late Aldo Rossi in 1983, an exceptional project to be inserted into a disparate and undistinguished landscape. The Palazzo lives up to its name, as haughty and majestic as a palace. Here, the windowless facade towers over the ungainly structures below it. Below, a pencil sketch by the architect showing a general view of the project, with the low buildings on either side opening onto interior streets.

Opposite page
A side facade, both rhythmic and rigorous: Iranian red brick, square windows with blue frames, and a bronze cornice that juts out below the roof.

To design a hotel that would go beyond the simple function of accommodation through an approach that was both social and cultural: that was the aim of Mitsuhiro Kuwasa in 1986, when he commissioned Aldo Rossi and Shigeru Uchida to build the Palazzo in Fukuoka, Japan. Highly enthusiastic about the project, the two architects, one Italian, the other Japanese, worked in constant collaboration, the first taking charge of the architectural design, the second supervising the artistic direction of the future establishment. Their three watchwords seem to have been: consistency, opacity, serenity. The architects wanted Il Palazzo to play a role in the reorganization of a disparate exterior landscape. They agreed that the building had to make an impact sufficiently powerful to mark the urban environment and sufficiently intemporal to resist the trends of passing fashion.

The name given to the future hotel is in itself a sign of its authors' intentions. The very word Palazzo evokes the idea

Repeated use of pure geometric forms, the circle and the square. With its rosy face in a steel rim, the clock is not merely decorative, but gives the accurate time to the many passersby.

Opposite page
One of the interior walkways, utterly plain and unadorned.

of luxury, with overtones of artistic and intellectual pursuits. It also places the project squarely within a European frame of reference. This European language was decisive when it became clear that the place destined to receive the hotel was to be a platform with a structural as well as a formal role. The space was divided on the basis of a constructive strategy with classical/renaissance reminiscences, expressed mainly by the differentiation of levels. The upper level contains floors 1 to 8, and the lower, in the shape of a horizontal prism, serves as a base for the hotel, containing the mezzanine and cellars. It also holds a group of public areas, such as the entertainment complex called Barna Crossing.

From each side of the entrance on this lower level, Italian style staircases lead to two modules parallel to the sides of the building. Here there are four bars, where people can move from the Russian atmosphere of El Obslomova by Shiro Kuramata to three other bars, designed by Gaetano Pesce, Ettore Sottsass and Rossi himself. Two interior streets separate the platform from these modules, the street of the Sun on the north, that of the Moon on the south. Delicate mosaics and diffuse lighting make walking through these streets particularly pleasant. Metal gangways link the modules to the upper part of the hotel.

The high, windowless facade gives the work all of its emblematic force and suggests a feeling both majestic and serene. This impression of tranquil strength is the fruit of a judicious blend of western classicism and oriental formalism. The architects chose a red brick from Iran whose intense color varies with the light and atmospheric conditions.

The vestibule is shared by a reception area and a large bar with a waiting area. The rhythmic pillars and soberly designed furniture contribute to creating a warm welcoming atmosphere, enhanced by the noble wall and ceiling coverings. The restaurant is reached by a simple marble entrance. Its decor, like its menu, is halfway between Italian and Japanese influences.

The design of the 62 guest bedrooms was entrusted to Ikuyo Mitsuhashi. With abundant allusions to both European and Asian style, he shows a constant search for discreet refinement, without ostentatious luxury or cumbersome decoration.

If the cultural fusion of the Asian and European worlds functions so naturally here, it is doubtless thanks to the personality of the two architects, both great names in the world of contemporary architecture. The work of Rossi, who

HOTEL
IL PALAZZO

28 Il Palazzo, Fukuoka, Japan

unfortunately died in a car accident in 1997, has won many awards, and includes such varied productons as The Conference Center of Milan, the Casa Aurora of Turin, the Galveston Arch and the Torri Center in Parma.

As for the Japanese designer Shigeru Uchida, his career has been distinguished over the years by the variety of his works as well as the exhibitions he has mounted around the world and the publication of specialized books. □

The geometry inspired by Gothic forms is used in this metal door, perfectly symmetrical with, once again, square and circle motifs.

Here, a watercolored sketch showing the solid facade with majestic colonnades and the deep color of the Iranian red brick.

Opposite page
If not for the furniture you might easily think you were in a Gothic chapel. The wall of glass bricks and the shimmer of the small lamps have a soothing effect on patrons who feel they are in a shrine rather than a bar.

Philippe Starck

Royalton

New York, United States

At the Royalton, as reinvented by Philippe Starck, everything is a game and every effect a piece of theater. From the very entrance, the two shiny metal handrails with their saucy curves seem to mock the haughty Ionic columns of the original neo-Grecian building.

Opposite page
A comfortable lounge area arranged under a glass roof and with a striking glass table as a centerpiece. The table legs double as flower vases, one of which holds a bouquet.

Philippe Starck is a magician, a sort of playful genie with a magic slate, without whom the landscape of the 1980s would have been singularly lacking in force and originality. The French playwright Sacha Guitry used to say: "Let us dream together..." an idea that Starck seems to echo wherever he creates. As he invents his surroundings, he invents us, too, with his constant concern for transforming life into a stage where all is possible, risky but desirable. All of his creations are marked by the same extreme exigence and magnificent optimism, which seem in the end to make the clientele feel elegant, natural and intelligent, as if some mysterious and inevitable alchemy took place between the set and the actors who occupied it for an hour or for a night.

It is hardly surprising therefore that the owners of the Royalton Hotel in New York thought of him for its renovation

Night life à la Philippe Starck. Above, the Royalton bar with its row of graceful if slightly bow-legged velvet stools, under another row of horn-shaped light fixtures. Perhaps the horns are meant to have a devilish look, a wink at the diabolical powers of the night for this otherwise very proper hotel.

Opposite page
Classic, curvaceous and comfortable – the booths seem conducive to intimate dining. An off-beat note is added by the tilted reflection and the strangle little tassel, made stranger by being seen twice.

in 1987. Ian Schrager and Steve Rubell, emblematic figures of New York night life in the 1980s (their Studio 54 and the Palladium revolutionized the disco and were imitated the world over) commissioned him to transform this building, dating from 1898, into an ultra-modern 5-star hotel. In accepting this challenge (it was the first time he was attempting a hotel project) Starck also wanted to reinvent something of what the Royalton had been in its day: "a hotel for people of some intelligence who belonged to creative or artistic milieu."

Starck focused his whole project for the refurbishment of the Royalton on the principle that the traveler is a person out of his shell who must be made to feel secure. From the lobby to the smallest element in the bathroom, each detail tries to be as comfortable as possible, a comfort that does not exclude humor, quite the contrary. For the spirit of trust to be created between the visitor and the space he will inhabit, the key point is quite obviously the bedroom. Deliberately decorated in an understated way, it welcomes the visitor with great simplicity and without ostentation. As soon as he sets foot in it, it seems to become his. In the center is the bed, made of mahogany and with good lighting that can be controlled with a simple flick of the wrist. It exudes comfort like an egg that our voyager will snuggle into. The other vector of well-being in the home is fire: home and hearth, as the expression goes. The largest rooms have a working fireplace with beautifully wrought accessories. In the others, a candlestick in a wall bracket is lit by the bell-boy when he carries in the luggage and hands you your keys, another detail to make you welcome. Next to the room the bath is treated like an alcove in pure and noble materials. Rough-textured stone on the floor, pleasant underfoot, contrasts with the smooth pale green walls and with the glitter of mirrors. These are set at a 45° angle to each other and add a note of fantasy by multiplying each object by four. The bathtub, nerve center of this refreshing grotto, is a round mini-pool, inviting the visitor for a welcome pause that restores the body and refreshes the senses.

On the ground floor the lobby stretches the entire block between 43rd and 44th Street. Starck has conceived it as a dynamic space in which a host of activities intertwine and interact. There are no television screens but guests can look into art books around a large rectangular table. A small half-hidden bar has a conspiratorial look that perfectly suits this designer's need to create mystery by teasing the curiosity of all present. This playfulness is also evident in the forms

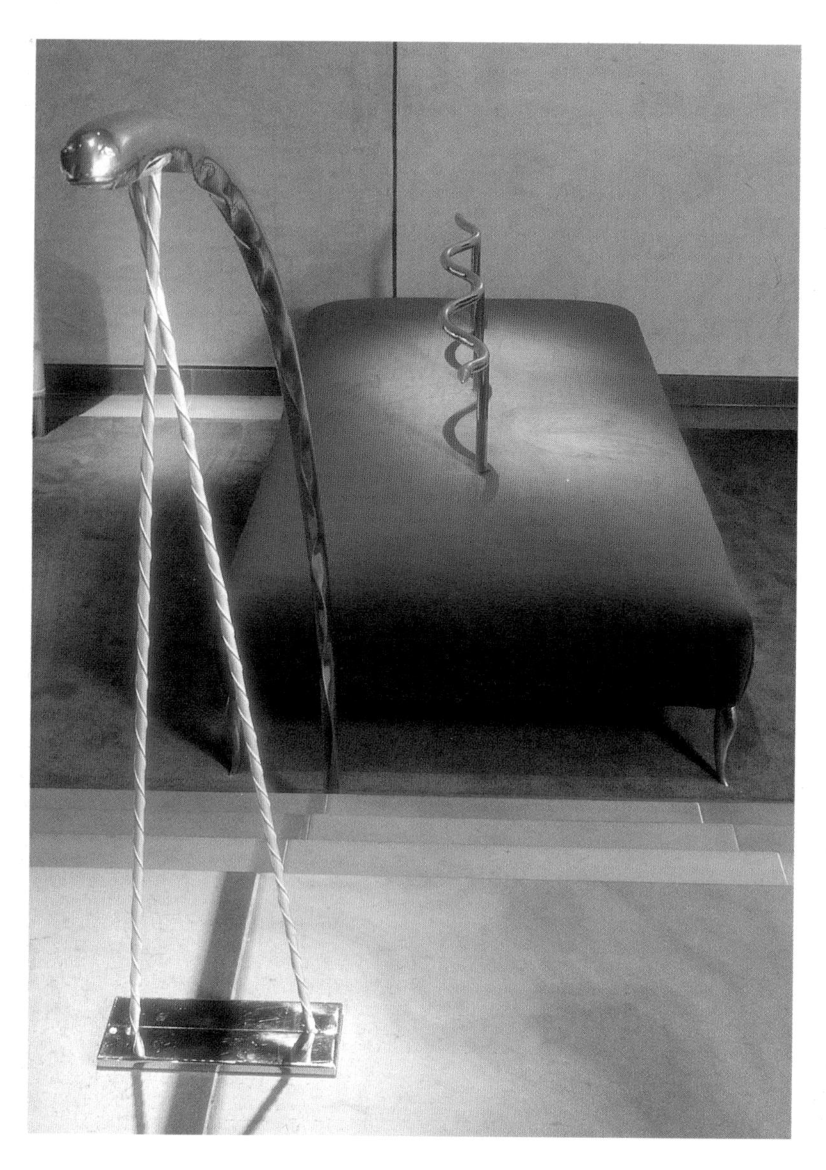

No, this is not King Arthur's sword plunged into the legendary stone! It is merely a sofa in the games area, where an ornamental serpent serves as a backrest and matches the serpent on the adjacent handrail.

An enigmatic sign inscribed in the hallway carpeting. Question mark or cabalistic symbol? Or just a sign questioning the vanity of all signs?

coming out of the walls, which look like a row of torches, or perhaps animal trophies, and in the sinuous railings with their serpent-like heads. The hallways, done in dark blue, are somber and recall Starck's nearly obsessive attachment to the theater. Enter any door, at random, and one finds that with each changing decor, the guest too can become another.

Starck likes to play games. Like all great creators, he is a manipulator. It is no surprise to find that the worlds he creates attract many artists, people who, like himself, are drawn to the image and the imaginary. □

View of the games room, with its strange atmosphere, half eerie, half playful, made of split levels, inclined planes and sinuous curves.

Here, a detail of the serpent's head that adorns the back rest of the sofa.

In the world according to Starck, there is always something thrown in to cut the theatrical effects, and to mock the traditional bourgeois interior such as this chaise longue in black leather and tubular steel. The oversized back rest bears some resemblance to an African ceremonial chair, or more prosaically, to an old-fashioned tin bathtub.

Opposite page
An elegantly draped curtain is gathered and held in place by a horn-shaped object that echoes the horns used elsewhere for light fixtures. The same shape is again parodied in the murally mounted flower vases.

The bathroom is a play of reflections and transparencies. A corner wash basin encased in glass and reflected in the glass walls, and the round tub that forms the center of an egocentric inner sanctum.

Opposite page
In the bedroom, less jest, more tranquility. The atmosphere is hushed and conducive to sweet repose.

Andrée Putman

Hotel im Wasserturm

Cologne, Germany

With the current awakening of interest in industrial architecture, an old water tower has been turned into a luxury hotel. The curve is the emblematic form of the building, here repeated in the reception desk, as it is everywhere in the hotel.

Opposite page
The Wasserturm at night: the massive cylinder of fine red brick with its rounded windows of varying size exerts a powerful presence. Only the topmost level has been rebuilt.

Every visitor to Cologne will come to admire the cathedral. But since 1990 the city boasts a new architectural curiosity that is not to be missed: a water tower converted into a luxury hotel. This feat was realized thanks to the talent of Andrée Putman and the result, though classic, is nonetheless completely original.

The 125-year-old structure served first as a water tower, before being turned into an air-raid shelter during World War II. The base escaped damage but the upper part of the tower was completely devastated and remained so until a renovation program began the work of restoration.

Today the Wasserturm is a most extraordinary hotel. In order to structure the inhabitable space it was necessary to design a complex architecture, involving unusual solutions. With 10 single rooms, 38 doubles and 42 suites (some of which have as many as 8 rooms), the hotel plays on the idea of the cylinder and endlessly repeats the motif of the circle. Light fixtures, side tables and doorknobs all display voluptuous curves. Several mezzanines and mirrored panels enlarge the space and endow it with great visual freedom. The bathrooms are intimate yet comfortable. Colored tiles, lots of mirrors and ample baths justify the Wasserturm's reputation for quality.

The structure, though industrial, borrows effects from the architectural world of the cathedral. The soaring volume is even more striking under the dramatic lighting, whose sculptural qualities are carefully calculated by Andrée Putman.

Opposite page
Looking downward at the corridors and walkways that lead to the bedrooms.

The integration of modern elements into the existing structure of an old brick building implies a new approach to space that anticipates the future. As soon as you enter the lobby you are immediately struck by a sentiment of both lightness and strength, not unlike the feeling projected by some religious buildings. Eleven meters high, this hall is organized with a subtle juxtaposition of slender pilasters and walkways. All in brick, it expresses both its attachment to history and its complete modernity. The choice of materials shows this constant wish to unite past and present with the combination of boldness and sobriety that characterizes all the work of this architect. Thus, in addition to the traditional brick made locally in the town of Frechen, we find more unusual materials, like African wood and rusted metal.

Andrée Putman's well-known attachment to contemporary art is expressed through the great number of works by artists characteristic of different styles of the period. A painting by American conceptual artist Donald Judd greets the visitor in the lobby, while in the restaurant the ceiling has been decorated by a pop-art painter, Tom Wesselmann. Nearly 350 paintings are offered up to the curiosity of the guests during their stay. Hung in every part of the hotel, including the guest bedrooms, works by such artists as Warhol, Baselitz, Immendorf, Penck and Vasarely contribute to creating the very particular atmosphere that reigns here.

There is a cushioned, insulated feel to many parts of the Wasserturm, with the exception of the glass-walled restaurant installed on the roof. Here diners can enjoy, in addition to the perfect service and high quality cuisine, a stupendous view of the city. Bright with sunlight by day, golden and intimate by night, this space, with its alternating glass, steel and tall luminous columns, distills a blond light imbued with magic. Broad sunny terraces offer a wonderful view of the famous cathedral. On these terraces the immaculate white accessories are set off by the pale green of well-placed vegetation.

Everywhere, tones of beige, yellow and bluish gray give the eye a quiet peaceful sensation. The old water tower right in the heart of town has lost none of its charm. Although its function has changed, it still remains an oasis of refreshment. □

The bar, showing the long curve of its illuminated counter.

The lounge looks cozy yet somewhat severe in the German manner. On the walls, drawings by contemporary artists, part of the collection of 350 works that are displayed in every part of the Wasserturm.

Opposite page
The rooftop terrace affords a breathtaking view over Cologne. The dining room itself is spacious and extremely classic, the only notes of fantasy, the luminous pillars and "daisy" patterned ceiling plaques.

The room is ringed by a wall of glass, with the open terrace forming a ring around which is a pleasant spot for sunbathing by day, or for romantic walks at night.

Sober, elegant and well-lit through the large, rounded windows, which form a central element for the interior architecture of the rooms. As for the furniture and draperies, they are smooth and uncluttered, in the style that Putman's has avowed for many years.
In the bathroom, the hand basin and accessories are ensconced in a gray tiled niche.

Opposite page
A corner of a lounge, where strong contrasts prevail between curves – the window contour, rug and low table – and straight lines – the stripes of the sofa and its high boxlike sides, one of which is further accentuated by a rectangular "window."

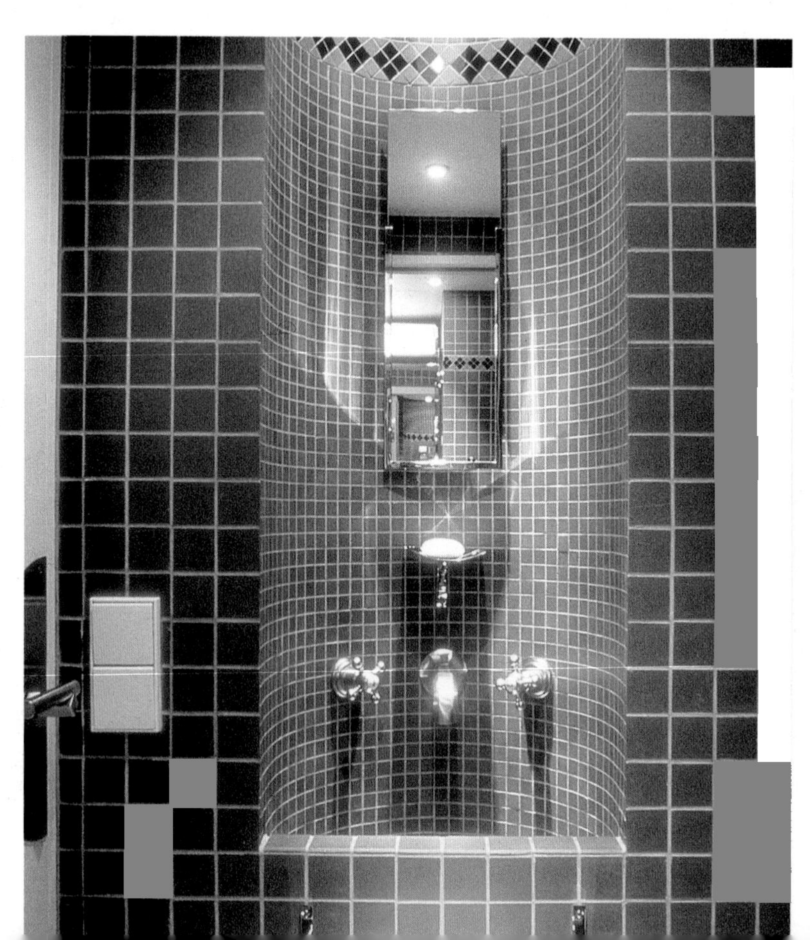

Marie-Christine Dorner

La Villa

Paris, France

The entrance area, in golden tones, seen through the front door, on which the name "La Villa" is inscribed in slender, stylized letters.

Opposite page
A complete change of palette in the bar – shades of blue and purple, violet and yellow, where the shape of the stairwell is oddly reminiscent of the signature hassock (the "pouf") of designer Marie-Christine Dorner.

The left bank Parisian quarter of St Germain-des-Prés is known as the haunt of artists and intellectuals, famous for its high style and beautiful people, its antique dealers, fashion boutiques, bars and restaurants, bookshops and publishers, and the famous cafés of the Deux-Magots, Flore and Lipp, where the elite like to meet. But behind the elegant boulevard beats the heart of an authentic village, with its narrow back streets, food markets and old cobblestones, all in the shadow of the ancient church tower, once part of the medieval abbey of St-Germain "in the Fields."

The hotel La Villa, on rue Jacob, is part of this neighborhood spirit. It is definitely a 4-star hotel, with all that the category implies, but its atmosphere is that of a real

The ever present "pouf" – an essential part of the decor. Seen here in red, matched and complemented by the carpet.

Figures of light projected on the floor – an efficient, not to mention poetic, way of indicating the room numbers, in the hushed, dimly-lit corridors.

A crisp, gleaming look for the bathroom, with a basin set into a broad oval table top.

For Marie-Christine Dorner, the bed is clearly the heart of room – even the ceiling curves gently over it as if to mark its importance. Here the ceiling is in red lacquer, affirming its Asian heritage.

A closer look at the "pouf" – its gently curving shape has an old-fashioned feel to it and the sensuality of color and texture confer great elegance.

Opposite page
A dressing table with its oddly-shaped mirror, not unlike a computer screen inspired by modern sculpture. The touch of violet coordinates it with the armchair, against a backdrop of almond green.

family home, a warm place, nice to come home to after a long night on the town, and in St Germain-des-Prés the nights don't end until the wee small hours...

This is the premise on which Marie-Christine Dorner has based the design of La Villa. Within the heart of the hotel, all has been done to favor sleep, with soft lighting and an atmosphere of stillness and repose. In the dimly-lit corridors a metal strip runs along the wall to prevent it from being scraped by passing suitcases. The room numbers are projected in numerals of light on the hallway floor. Inside each room, the epicenter, the focal point, is the bed. The ceiling is designed to be seen, to be contemplated, a reference to an age-old tradition in Asia. Here at La Villa, it is covered with taffeta, in cool tones of deep blue, turquoise or almond green, and turns down over the walls. The curtains are of the same taffeta, falling in stiff, heavy folds, looking almost as if they were starched. They highlight the volume and confirm the feeling of being in a sheltered alcove.

The furniture – leather hassock and armchair, coffee table and side tables, desk and light fixtures – is all signed Marie-Christine Dorner. So are the quilted and beribboned bedspreads. In the bathroom, a chrome basin with a center of frosted glass and a little waterfall bubbling from it serves as a water fountain. The same quiet ambience pervades the entire hotel, with one exception. The bar is the one place set apart from the tranquil spirit of the rest. Here, with violet carpets and chairs of garnet-colored leather, shades of red envelop the late-night crowd, who come to listen to the jazz that the Villa features all year long. And quality jazz at that, with the solid and melodious rhythms of bassist Scott Colley.

So even those who have no intention of sleeping at the hotel can spend an evening in what has become one of the best swinging clubs of St Germain des Prés. □

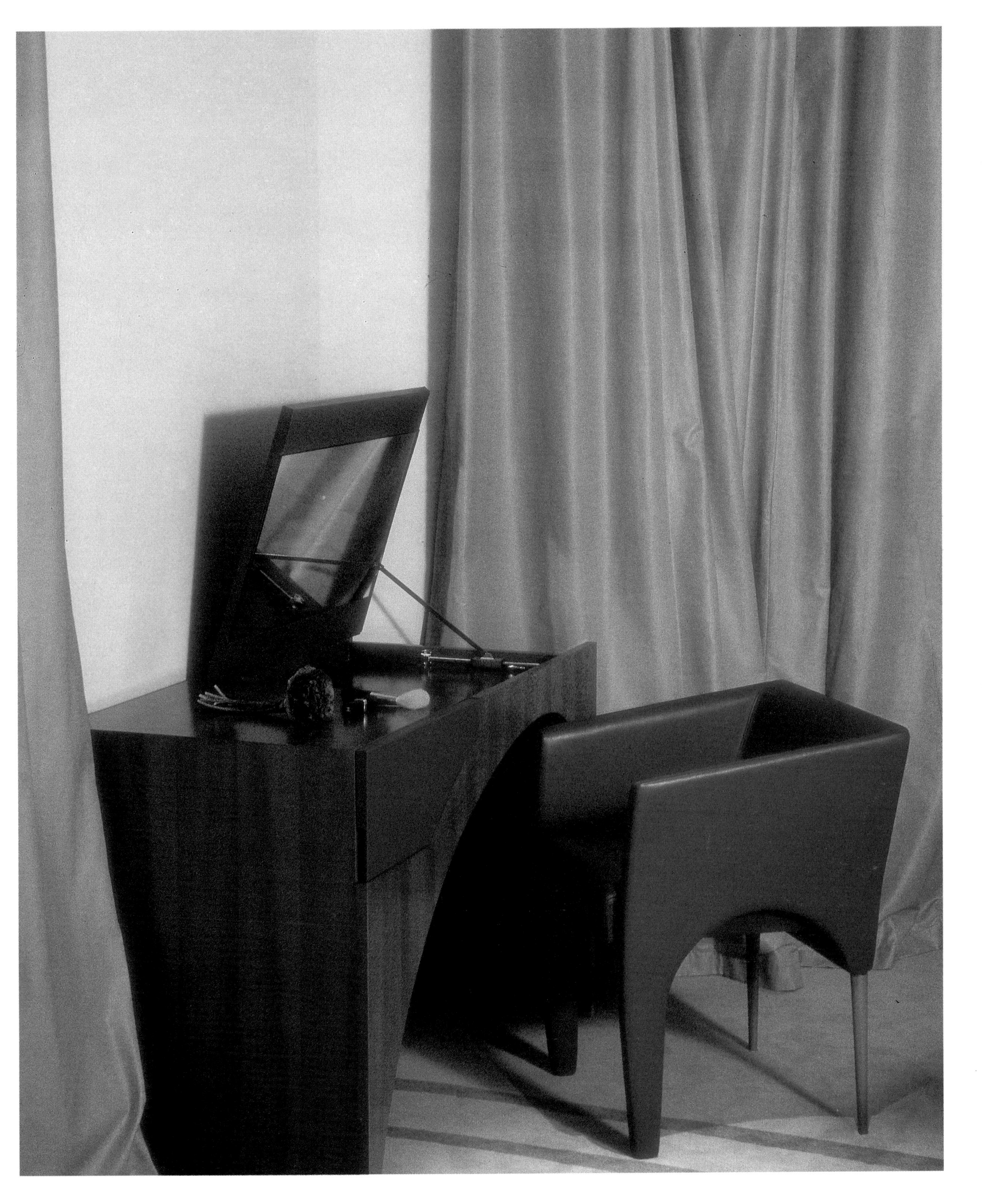

Twin wash basins of shiny chrome adorn the bathroom, each topped with its three-sided mirror.

Opposite page

Violet and almond green are the leading colors in this scenography that hints somehow of the mysterious Orient. The two giant bows on the bedspread add a girlish touch.

Dirk Obliers

Pflaums Posthotel

Pegnitz, Germany

From the outside, no one would ever know that Pflaums Posthotel was anything other than a typical Bavarian inn. A former postal hotel, it comes complete with half-timbered facade and big clumps of geraniums in the window boxes. But inside, it is a real Pandora's box. It is only a few kilometers from Bayreuth, and architect Dirk Obliers has made it into an homage to Richard Wagner, as well as to his own techno-kitsch fantasies.

Opposite page
The "Lichttunnel", a "tunnel of light" that leads to an interior golf course.

When two confirmed nonconformists, a designer and a hotel owner, come together, the result is rarely disappointing. When in addition the encounter takes place on a terrain imbued by the spirit of Richard Wagner, we can imagine the eccentricities we are in for.

In the case of Pflaums Posthotel Pegnitz, however, nothing one could imagine quite comes up to the reality. Undoubtedly, the proximity of Bayreuth, home of the famous Wagner Festival, was an added source of inspiration for fantasy or at least for allusions to the tumultuous world of Wagner and his patron Louis II of Bavaria. At Pflaums the reference is not just an allusion, it is a complete immersion. No effort has been spared, no detail overlooked, to plunge the hotel guests into a completely new world, with no concrete link to the mundane universe they've left outside. Designer Dirk Obliers has everywhere provided treats for the eye. It is through the eyes that a child marvels at the world and accedes to fantasy and dream.

In the lobby a gigantic screen presents non-stop excerpts from great Wagnerian productions while peepholes along the walls offer a glimpse of the sumptuous decoration of

"Orpheus Plays Golf" is the title of this dreamlike construction. On the right, the bar of the suite named "Parsifal."

Opposite page
For Dirk Obliers, every bedroom is a stage. In this one, "Tristans Traumeslust", the alcove around the bed is made with the decors of *Tristan and Isolde,* Act I, painted by Max Bückner for the performance of 1886.

different rooms or suites in the hotel. These are named for the master's works, the "Parsifal Suite" with its metallic, geometric, futuristic decor, the "Venus in Blue Suite," treated like an oasis, with particular care given to the lighting (the ceiling is said to be an exact copy of the stars in an arctic sky) the "Tristan Suite," all in red velvet with a bedstead richly bedecked in fabrics of gold and midnight blue. In such a decor, who could avoid the most extravagant dreams? It is no wonder that so many celebrities have stayed in these enchanting suites.

From Michael Jackson to the Emperor of Japan, from Placido Domingo to John Travolta, there is no end to the famous names who have relaxed in the "Black Grotto", an immense jacuzzi surmounted by a kaolin vault where 2,000 tiny spotlights bring out reflections in the granite. A "White Suite," more restful to the eye, will please those who prefer classicism and sobriety. But here too a state-of-the-art sound system lets them listen till all hours as lovely Isolde weeps her love for Tristan.

Dirk Obliers has achieved this magical, fairy tale world through a constant striving to consider each space as the theater of new experiences. One of the keys to his success

Two gentler versions of luxury
according to Pflaums: one called
"Klingsors Zaubergarten," above,
based on a variety of motifs
using wood; and the other, a
dream all in white,
"Weisse Suite."

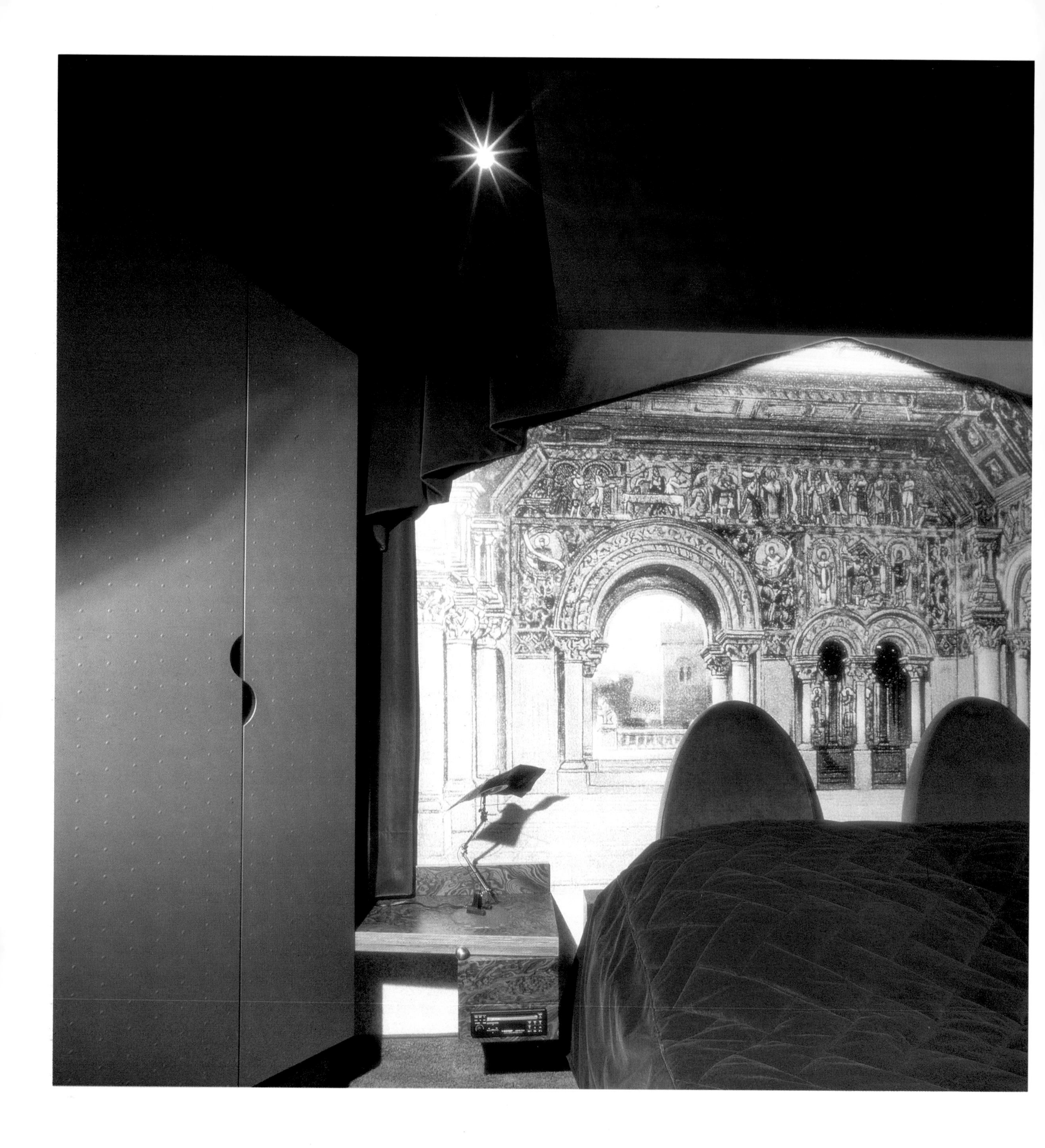

62 Pflaums Posthotel, Pegnitz, Germany

is based on a wish to create an immediate and permanent dialogue between guest and decor. Particularly attentive to all that concerns lighting, he has also designed and made most of the furnishings for the rooms and baths. This exacting designer combines unusual materials with strong clear ideas, following through to the smallest details. All together, it adds up to a perfect and powerful identity that leaves a strong mark on the imagination of the guests, and it is they who become the hotel's main ambassadors.

It is clear that the Pfaulms is in a class by itself in the hotel world. This former postal inn directed by the four Pflaum brothers carries the cult of Wagner into the restaurant as well. There are menus called "Trilogy" or "Quadrilogy" and one savory morsel offered as an overture is named Wagnerian Ode to foie gras.

Anyone who has stumbled in by accident and can't abide the pomp of the *Meistersinger* can always stay in the older part of the hotel, replete with Biedermeier charm, where the spirit of Rossini, Donizetti or Weber will perhaps come to them in their rooms. But then again, what would anyone who's not a Wagner buff be doing so close to Bayreuth? □

The "Bacchanal Suite," with a bedroom once more like a stage set, this time from *Tannhaüser,* Act II. For the living room area, a coy arrangement all in plush velvet, somewhere between Pigalle and Baby Doll.

The "Parsifal Suite." On the opposite page the hero's cavern in a style resembling a child's building toy construction, with metal parts, mirrors and luminous fiber. Here, the bathroom, a mixture of colored slate and sheet metal. Below, another childlike setting called the "hall of games" with toy cars and magnets on the walls.

Toyo Ito

Hotel Poluinya

Hokkaido, Japan

High surrounding walls forming a perfect oval rising from the water, with a long covered walkway, like a vestibule, leading inward to the protected heart of the complex. The Poluinya is an enclave insulated from its environment.

Opposite page
Lines and veins in relief with the reflections of light and water: the poetry of geometry from the hand of Toyo Ito.

Like some closed-off autonomous territory, the Hotel Poluinya rises over the vast grain fields of Hokkaido. With only 26 rooms, the hotel created by Toyo Ito nevertheless boasts all the comfort expected in an establishment of its category.

The layout of the Poluinya is extremely simple: two levels are allocated to the guest bedrooms and one is set aside for the common areas, largely the reception area and the restaurant. This common part, oval in shape, is surrounded by high walls that seem to isolate the hotel from the outside world, thus accentuating the idea of a protected zone, independent of the natural environment around it. The high concrete walls rise like two enormous parentheses that capture the reflections of the sun. This toying with the surrounding nature only reinforces the hotel's resolutely urban appearance. The confrontation between town and country functions in complete harmony, the screenlike walls protecting the inner parts of the hotel from the seasonal rains prevalent in the fields around. It is like an abstraction of a city planted in a country landscape, an ultra-modern figure, artificial yet perfectly integrated.

Parallel to the oval public space, the two levels of rooms seem to create a trench 70 meters long; all of glass and steel, stretched out across the plain. Each of the 26 rooms has a

wonderful view of Mount Shari to the southeast. Inside, the comfort of the facilities matches the impression of sobriety that defines the site. Everything you need is there, yet nothing is ostentatious or overdone.

Linearity, rigor of forms and materials all contribute to the general feeling of peace and transparency, further enhanced by the materials used – industrial glass, steel and concrete. With the reflections of light on the various surfaces and the mirror effects they create, the hotel seems to surge up like a motionless vessel, the interior remaining opaque to the exterior, encapsulating the clients in an intimate and protected world.

The name "Poluinya" comes from the Russian term designating a place amid glaciers, where water does not freeze. No wonder that Toyo Ito's hotel has the look of an enclave. □

The entrance lobby: like the exterior, the interior makes use of ample space and great sobriety.

Opposite page
The hotel consists of an oval containing the public areas and an elongated block that holds the 26 rooms. The northwest face is solid and unbroken, while the southeast facade, as shown above in a closer view, has a view of Mount Shari and the fields of Hokkaido.

The bar opening onto a patio.

Preceding pages
At the Poluinya, graphics replaces color. The flowing parallels induce a feeling of well-being and serenity.

One of the bedrooms: flooded with light and with an ample view of the landscape.

Dorine De Vos

Hotel New York

Rotterdam, The Netherlands

For nearly 100 years now, the Hotel New York has stood on the docks of Rotterdam, looking out to sea. Its massive brick walls, well weathered by sea spray, have sheltered generations of travelers bound for America.

Opposite page
A vast ballroom where crystal chandeliers from bygone days mingle happily with modern lighting and exposed pipes, against a vividly-colored background.

A person who travels is a person away from home... An observation as simple (or simplistic) as this one may suffice to begin a train of thought that can arouse a hotel designer to accomplish some pretty ambitious projects. Viewed through the prism of this definition, a hotel client is someone deprived of his traditional landmarks. In this fragile condition he becomes an ideal subject of study for designers, whose profession, after all, consists first and foremost of putting themselves in the place of others and in modeling the space around them.

In this regard, the great obstacle for the three designers commissioned to refurbish Rotterdam's Hotel New York was the hotel's past, heavy with the weight of history. The massive brick building had once belonged to the steamship company the Holland-Amerika Lijn. It had witnessed the passage of a host of immigrants leaving the old world, whether by choice or obligation, all bound for America and dreams of a better life. The vast rooms of the edifice, built between 1901 and 1917, must have heard their share of laughter and tears, held the memories of joy and despair.

Dorine de Vos, in charge of coordinating the project, naturally took this heritage into account in the conception of the work. To recreate a hotel without nostalgia but inspired

by the past, to revive the hospitality and elegance of the voyages of yesteryear, this was the challenge that faced her. The hotel boasts 72 rooms, five large halls, a fine terrace, and a restaurant open on the sea, where natives of Rotterdam cross paths with hotel guests. A new room installed in one of the hotel's two towers and a luxury suite available for longer stays were designed with the same care as in the rest of the project. Woodwork of walnut and rosewood and Art Nouveau rugs designed by the Dutch designer Colenbrander and renovated by the Tilburg textile museum add a touch of refinement in perfect harmony with the configuration of the hotel. With its balconies, the corner towers with the multi-faced clocks, the Jugendstil motifs and slightly offbeat symmetry, the building had a strong personality that had to be reckoned with. Set down like some great ship docked amid the expanse of wharves, with its two landmark towers, the building itself seems ready to put out to sea, hesitating endlessly between setting sail and staying where it is moored.

The dual constraint imposed on Dorine De Vos and her team was to work within a short time and a tight budget, making it necessary to rigorously weigh each proposal. Their modest claim is that they have merely designed the sort of space they would themselves like to find if they landed in a place like this, a vague no-man's-land that looks as if it came out of a Spilliaert painting. In fact Dorine De Vos designed not only the interiors but all the graphics, down to the staff uniforms and landscape modeling. White for the bedding, heavy drapery on the walls, marine charts and model ships

View of the hotel from the esplanade on the day of its inauguration.

The Art Nouveau staircase adorned with teal blue carpeting.

Opposite page
The spacious restaurant also plays on contrasts: chandelier and little spotlights, simple decor and panoramic view.

A lecture hall has an unfinished look... as if to suggest an imminent departure.

New York
Labrador
CANADA
Quebec
Philadelphia
Baltimore
C. Charles
Chesapeake Bay
Norfolk
Georgetown
Charleston
COMPANY
ROTTERDAM
AMSTERDAM
NEW YORK
CHICAGO
BOULOGNE SUR MER
LONDON

HNY
044

G BASELITZ

against colored paneling, the atmosphere a constant blend of cruise ship and theatrical set. The attention paid to each detail is not just for appearances' sake. It is part of a larger view that consists of defining an identity, of rooting an atmosphere in the traveler's mind. "What is in the cup is as important as the line of the cup itself, or what it stands on or the look of the person carrying it. In the same way, the appearance of the waiter is inseparable from the design of the table on which he places the cup or the chair in which the client is sitting. In short, it's all one, all image and atmosphere. Theater!"

Set at the edge of a zone in process of complete transformation, where private homes, business complexes and shopping centers are gradually being installed, the Hotel New York of Rotterdam (one of the most dynamic port cities of Europe) is a proud link between past and future. And the guest seated behind the large windows and gazing out over the docks and the sea will know that one need not go far away in order to travel. □

In one room, unmatched furniture, packing cases, stippled walls – could it be that we're already on board ship? Another is more stolid – surely we are still in Rotterdam, but the voyage begins at the window sill. Yet another, with old-fahsioned woodwork, a dressing table picked up at an antique sale, and an odd two-tone chair, seems borrowed from many times, many places...

Jean Nouvel

Hôtel Saint-James

Bouliac, France

Opposite page
Inside, the hotel decor uses soft tones of gray, blond and caramel, which have a sensual glow when caressed by the light.

Smack in the middle of a vineyard, the Saint-James gently thumbs its nose at protocol and at all the "proper" conventions of the hotel trade. The meshwork of the facades seems to borrow its color and hardy appearance from the surrounding earth and vines.

From a distance, particularly at close of day, when the sun shining on the rusted forms seems to set them ablaze, the surprised traveler will be tempted to check his map to be sure he's in the right place. Are these tobacco sheds? Or disused barns? Set down amid the vines, the series of volumes stands lined up like Monopoly houses on the heights of Bordeaux. It is an intriguing, not to say a baffling spectacle. But checking his map our traveler will see that this is indeed Bouliac and these strange forms illuminated by the setting sun are indeed the Hôtel Saint-James, the place he has set out to sleep in.

And so we approach. We let ourselves be drawn in. Slowly the surprise gives way to a desire to abandon all free will and enter this new and unexpected world. All at once, the fact that this hotel looks nothing like a hotel enchants us. We smile at our initial reaction, at the momentary hesitation that tempted us to head for town, back to the familiar look of old stone. But here we are. We've parked the car and contemplate the scene, suddenly convinced that the old stones can wait. The buildings stand before us, looking rather like corn cribs wrapped in rusty gauze, and drawing us in with the insolence of their modernity. In the distance, the town over the Garonne is no more than an uncertain blur

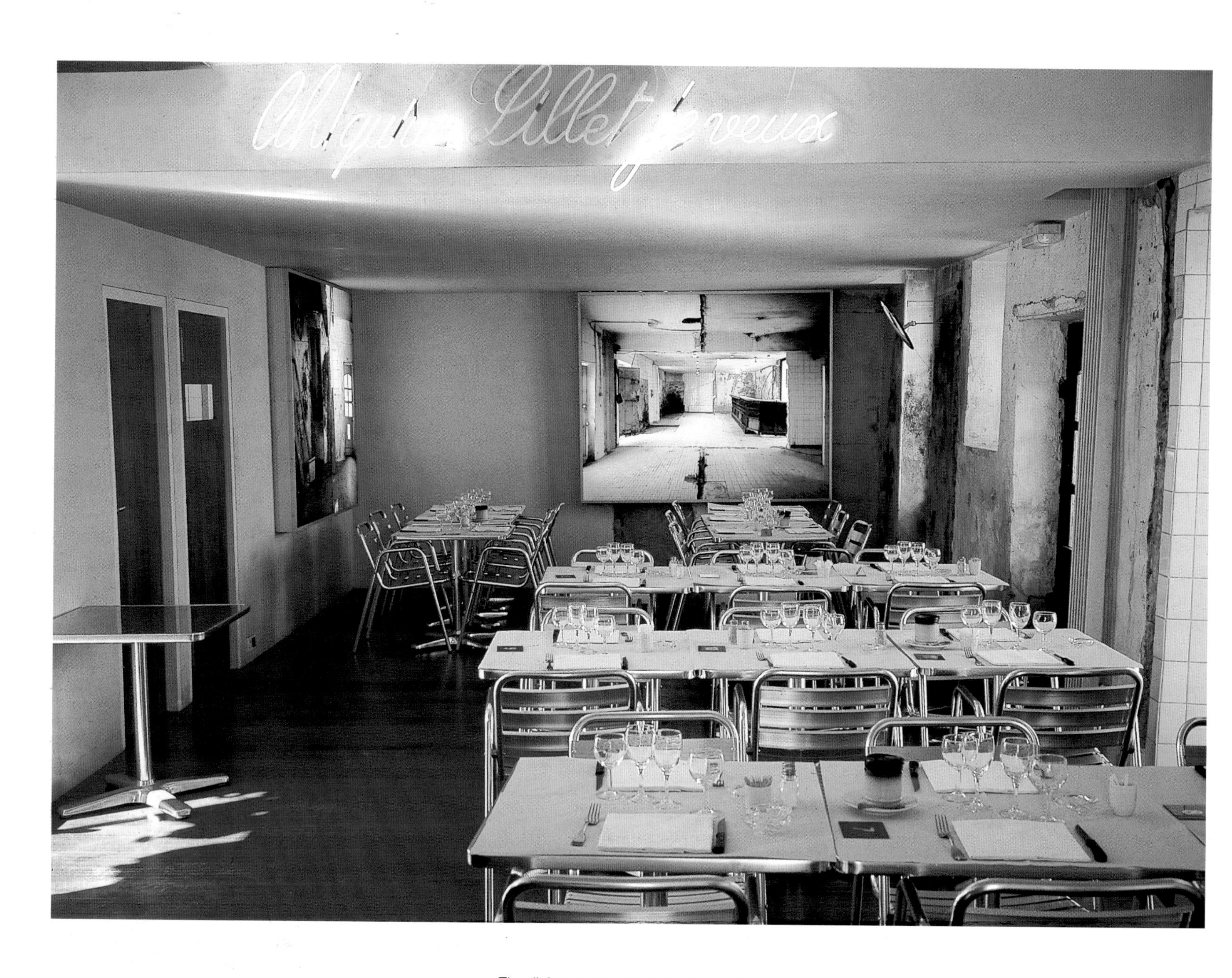

The dining room, with its luminous sign advertising a brand of aperitif. As for the rest the decor (or absence thereof) it seems to imitate a roadside rest stop... or a school cafeteria.

Opposite page
The Saint-James boldly borrows from vernacular architecture. The rusted metal coverings that at first glance seem crude and unfinished, in fact give birth to a startling variety of textures – checked, cross-hatched or perforated.

waiting for nightfall. This stunning view is the raison d'être of the Hôtel Saint-James and the power that dictated to Jean Nouvel the inner organization of the space. It is the constant partner that commands, imposes. As soon as the eye takes in the unique landscape, we realize that it could not have been any other way. It comes as no surprise to learn that every one of the hotel's 18 rooms enjoys a 180° view on the mellow and shimmering valley.

The rusted mesh of the facades gives no hint of the blond and luminous softness that reigns inside. The rigorously contemporary lines in no way preclude the comfort and serenity that is the aspiration of any traveler worthy of the name. In the rooms, oblique white walls, polished concrete floors, blond wood bed frames and modern lighting are in perfect harmony with the stainless steel and enamel of the bathrooms. The furniture is functional, including steel-based tables and, in the restaurant, Spirou chairs with removable covers. The beds, most of them with headboards, are set out in such a way that the guest can contemplate the view to his heart's content. In this way, each room functions as kind of a luxury module totally dedicated to the surrounding panorama. The bare walls do not distract the eye and the landscape of vineyards can be savored like a fine wine.

Whether the guest is a tourist or a professional traveler or a pilgrim come to drink in the charm and mystery of the surroundings, the test of a fine hotel is its ability to reconcile the traveler with the passing time.

For all its modernity, the Hôtel Saint-James leaves a strange impression of immutability in the traveler's mind, as if this ancient winegrowing region had transmitted to the atmosphere of the place some ancestral secrets of conviviality and quiet contentment. Perhaps that is why, despite its mere 10 years of existence, this hotel designed by Jean Nouvel seems enriched by an added memory we often fail to find in much older establishments.

And perhaps it is just this dimension of memory that will make us want to return some day to this memorable Saint-James at Bouliac. □

The vineyard slopes down toward the town of Bouliac beside the Garonne. This panoramic view, visible from everywhere in the hotel, is in fact the principal element of decoration.
The vines come right up to the swimming pool. Even here, you can't forget you're in wine country.

Above and following
pages: behind the
slatted window blinds,
a spacious bedroom,
sparely decorated in
pale, cool colors. The
white covers give a
functional, "no-frills"
look. From the beds,
which face the broad
windows, the view
extends, by day or by
night, as far as
eye can see.

Wolfgang Döring

Dom Business Hotel

Düsseldorf, Germany

Built in the heart of Grafenberg Forest, the Dom Business Hotel is a verdant oasis of calm just a few kilometers from Düsseldorf. Wolfgang Döring has based the construction of his hotel, both inside and out, on simple geometric shapes like the cylinder, cube and pyramid. One square building and one round one contain in all 59 rooms (37 singles and 22 doubles).

You enter the Dom through a lobby 8 meters high, where a bar and a monumental fireplace greet the visitor and add to the atmosphere of hospitality. The lobby is lit by a glass pyramid. The impression of homogeneity you feel from the very first is due to the fact that the architect designed it all, down to the smallest details. From the elevator cabins to the shape of the tables and lamps, Döring has left nothing to chance, aware that this was the sine qua non if the identity of the Dom was to conform to his wishes. In the guest bedrooms as well as the public areas, the key words are simplicity and rigor. In the round part of the hôtel the rooms are semi-circular and offer traditional facilities, highlighted with easily identifiable contemporary furniture. The Le Corbusier chairs, to cite just one example, set a tone of classic modernity.

The dining room is simple and spacious. With it broad glazed front it offers a fine view of the 15 hectares (over 30

Opposite page
The brightly reflecting pillars give a slender, soaring feel to the structure.

A modern version of the trellis serves as entrance to a new and graphic universe, while waiting for its covering of vines, clematis and climbing roses.

Ringed by trees, this modern chateau stands in the twilight, an elegant silhouette with its windows and pinnacle borrowed from tradition.

acres) of grounds. In the evening, with the trees illuminated, it is a spectacle both noble and restful. In the same wish for consistency, the architect participated in the choice of dishes and silverware and in the decoration of the tables.

A fitness and relaxation center has been installed in the basement. A wonderful swimming pool (with a zen-like aura) in a white-tiled space offers the possibility of a swim between two business meetings. Around the pool, white pillars enlarge the space and multiply the perspectives.

With a wish to integrate the hotel into the surrounding landscape, Döring has covered a large part of the outer walls with trellises, on which climbing plants will eventually find a home. An effective way to recall that the Dom stands in the heart of a protected site. A manner also of giving guests from the city the illusion that the Grafenberg Forest in person is inviting them to come and enjoy a stay filled with the murmur of the foliage and the song of the birds. □

Above: detail of the cleverly designed light fixtures in perforated metal.
Left: scale model of the Dom.

The cathedral effect. Above and right, the interior design of the bar has an almost "gothic" look, playing with symmetry and reflections, sober and orderly. Wolfgang Döring chooses the clean lines of Le Corbusier chairs and a motif of graceful perforations.

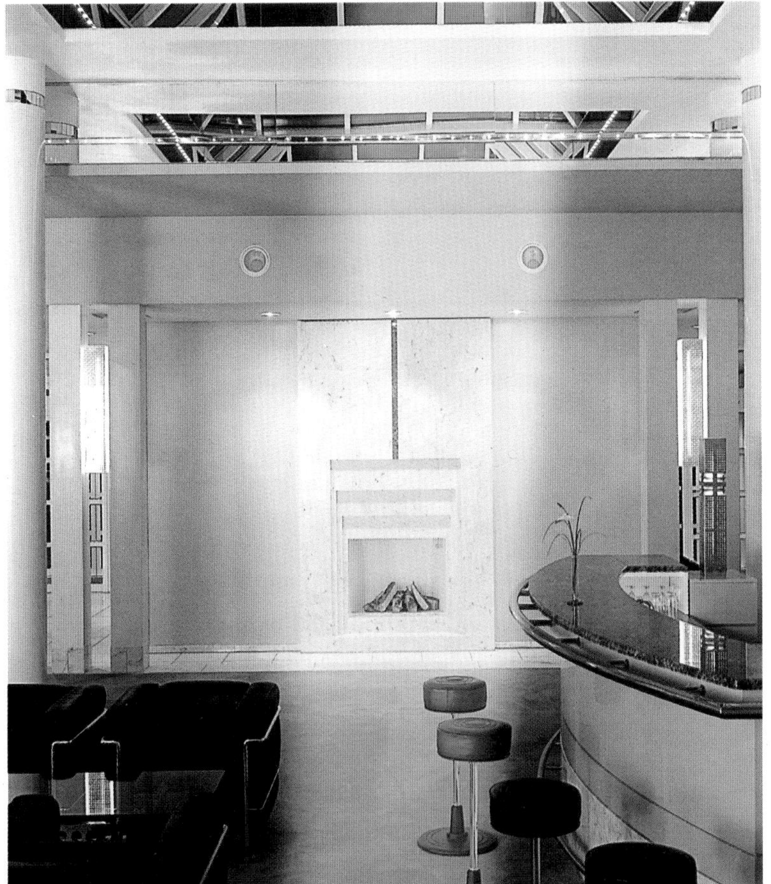

The swimming pool, in a restful and meditative setting, is on the floor below.

Hans Pösinger

Der Teufelhof

Basel, Switzerland

The tentlike structure set up in the courtyard shelters an improvised dining room where guests can eat outdoors in summer. The name Teufelhof means "devil's courtyard," but the hotel is more like a guardian angel... to artists, that is.

There are many ways to initiate the public to contemporary art or to creation in a wider sense. In a hotel it is always possible to reserve a space for exhibitions that the clients can regard with a more or less attentive eye, while waiting to sign in or get a taxi. But experience proves these spaces more often evoke the dullness of a waiting room than the dynamic feel that is or should be projected by an art gallery.

At Der Teufelhof in Basel the idea they found to promote art and culture is an audacious one, for the initiation takes place in the rooms themselves. This hotel wants to serve as a kind of link between its guests and the world of contemporary creation. To that end it has opened each of its eight rooms to the fantasy of an artist, whose work appears on the walls and ceiling of the room. The artists are given free reign, the only criterion imposed on them being to ensure a level of comfort commensurate with a three-star hotel. The main advantage of such an experiment lies in the intimacy, even complicity created between the work and the visitor. Unlike a gallery that one walks through, paying more or less attention, the fact that this is a room one sleeps in makes the relationship a deeper and more normal one. The

Indoor dining takes place in the very proper dining room, one of the more conventional looking parts of the hotel.

guest, living in close contact with the works, begins to take them as part of his normal surroundings. They cease to be exceptional pieces about which he is obliged to form an opinion, to make a judgment, but become as ordinary as the other furnishings of the rooms, the tv, radio or refrigerator.

For all the originality of the idea, the experience might have become monotonous if it had not been decided from the outset to completely refurbish the rooms every two years. New artists, new works, total transformation of all eight rooms. How else to stimulate the curiosity that is at the very heart of this experiment? Using collages, mobiles, lighting effects and trompe-l'œil, painters and plastic artists, undoubtedly excited by the innovative character of the idea, threw themselves whole-heartedly into the project. What artist has not dreamed that some passer-by, a stranger in the night, should cast a new eye on his work just on awakening? With furniture by Kurt Thut or Magistretti and Castiglioni, being in such good company can only favor productive interaction.

The traditional style "Weinstube," a wine garden surrounded by greenery.

Those of the rooms that are not designed by artists are simply and tastefully decorated, spacious and comfortable as well.

More traditional in appearance is this room with its attic roof and beams, done in marbled blue.

Opposite page
Lyrical lines that look as if they come from the hand of a genie playing with a crayon of light. Rooms number 4 and 8 by Swiss artists Ruth Handschin and Teres Wydler.

In other parts of the hotel, gastronomy and culture also live well together. The hotel boasts two reputed restaurants and two theaters, the larger of which, with a capacity of nearly 100, has been fitted out with the former seats of the Zurich Opera. The programming is both classical and eclectic. "Not just for fun, but also for reflection..." say the organizers seriously.

Recently, the hotel was enlarged by a 20-room annex including four very comfortable suites. This gallery hotel continues the vocation of its elder, for the entire building is intended to serve the creation of a painter, sculptor or plastic artist. Different works by the same artist are displayed throughout the rooms, hallways and reception area.

Gastronomy, theater and culture. By mixing these three modes, Monica and Dominique Thommy-Kneschaurek, who run the Teufelhof, hope to encourage a "free circulation" between genres, so that gourmets may discover the theater, avant-gardists fine food and Shakespeare-lovers the unknown talent of a Pollock of tomorrow. Lest the ordinary mortal be frightened by such an outpouring of culture, let us reassure him with the reminder that at the Teufelhof you can, if you like, do nothing more taxing than rest. □

Stripped down to the barest minimum – two beds, light to read by, a window with a bucolic view, and on the walls, an artist's creation that evokes a fissured wall, or the coastline of some imaginary land, or anything the beholder chooses to make of it.

In room number 3, signed Brigitte Kordina, a sprinkling of torn paper hovers magically over the bed. The guest's imagination does the rest: is it a mobile? an origami construction? the pieces of a torn love letter?
Left: view over the rooftops of Basel, through a casement window taken straight from the local architecture. The furniture here is by Italian designers Vico Magistretti and Achille Castiglioni.

Burkhalter and Sumi

Hotel Zürichberg

Zürich, Switzerland

From one world to another. At the end of the corridor that links the new addition to the hotel by architects Burkhalter and Sumi (opposite page) to the older section designed by Streiff and Schindler (below), a flight of wooden steps and the fanlike folds of a protruding wall.

Located on the heights of Zürich, the Hotel Zürichberg, built by the architects Streiff and Schindler in 1911, was classified as a Historic Monument in 1990. The work of remodeling the hotel was given to Marianne Burkhalter and Christian Sumi, after they had won a competition for an enlargement project in 1989.

The hotel's status of historic landmark reoriented their approach to the project and made them decide to build a new part, independent of the old. This new section, with a facade of Canadian wood, stands to the west of the original building and is connected to it only at the rear. Its low rounded shape contrasts markedly with the "house in the country" style of the old one. However, the old part remains the nerve center of the hotel, with all organized around it.

A number of changes were made in the original hotel to respond to the structural imperatives connected to the addition of the annex, which was to contain 72 parking

The new wing of the Zürichberg: a spiral consisting of two levels of rooms and a 72-space parking garage underneath.

Opposite page
The curved corridor that connects the two parts of the hotel.

spaces and 30 rooms. The main consequence of this transformation lies in the relation of building to terrain. The base on which the building used to stand is now gone, which puts the hotel in direct contact with the garden. The visitor entering the reception area can accede directly to the terrace, from which he has a magificent view of Zürich and the chain of the Alps. All the rooms surrounding the reception have been restored in total respect of their original appearance. The search for unity is also visible in the way the bedrooms and baths were redesigned with an eye to preserving their typical turn-of-the-century charm.

The need to create a vast parking space was a prime element behind the project, which was conceived in the form of an oval ramp, like a "screw boring into the earth." With three levels devoted to parking and two to the hotel,

the new building is like a spiral linked to the original structure by a corridor, a cylindrical passage situated at the garden level. Deliberately without a private entrance in order to reinforce its appearance of isolated object, this annex is perfectly integrated in the landscape, particularly as the entrances to the parking area have been built on the north side, thus invisible from the garden.

In the hotel part, the lighting is dispensed through the horizontal windows on the sides and a skylight on the roof, creating a pleasant atmosphere that changes according to the time of day and color of the season. Particular care has been taken with the color scheme. It scrupulously respects the tones of the original facade, varying from pale yellow to rust red and harmoniously complemented by the warm tints of the different kinds of wood. The green of the original shutters has been used again for the shutters of the new building, as well as for the roof and gravel of the paths. To reinforce the structural unity, the same range of colors has been used inside and out.

The actual interior design varies between the old and new parts. The renovated rooms of the original hotel respect the traditional style, whereas in the 30 new rooms the furnishings are more varied and flexible. Mobile screens and strongly stylized furniture (Alvar Aalto armchairs, Shaker style tables...) give each space a personality of its own. Beautiful oak parquet floors add warmth with their rich dark brown color, another manner of anchoring this annex in tradition without ever denying the resolutely modern style of the architects. □

A pair of armchairs signed Alvar Aalto, a small fragile-legged table and the light coming through the slats of the window blinds combine to give a feeling of grace and delicacy.

Opposite page
Above: the furniture repeats the color scheme of the exterior structure, black, brick and cream.
Below: the well-balanced arrangement of verticals and horizontals on the gentle curve of the building.

Philippe Starck

Mondrian

Los Angeles, United States

The Mondrian, inside and out: the first glimpse is of the monumental lobby, all in orange hues.

Opposite page
Dining takes place under this extraordinary arbor bordered by oversized terra cotta flower pots and roofed with trellises bearing (with the changing seasons) bougainvillea, gardenia, jasmine, rosemary or honeysuckle... The chairs are of teak with green or yellow canvas backs, which look very much at home in the dappled light that enters through the foliage.

Every time Philippe Starck and Ian Schrager set out on a new adventure, they seem like two old playmates launching into a new game. The Mondrian, the latest fruit of their long and fertile collaboration, which began with Morgans in New York, is no exception. Here too they exhibit the desire to draw visitors into a sort of game, where humor, magic and surprise are always intermingled.

Located on prestigious Sunset Boulevard, the building dates from 1959 and was converted into a hotel in 1984. What differentiates Schrager's hotels from all the others is a prevalent feeling of no holds barred, anything goes. Enough of those hotels cum dormitories where you return at night only to sleep.

A hotel as Schrager and Starck see it – from Morgans to the Royalton, from the Paramount to the Delano in Miami – is like an experimental field based on the notion that life is a game. Games are needed to stimulate the senses and make the spirit soar. But this love of fantasy would probably not

110 Mondrian, Los Angeles, United States

suffice if it were not accompanied by a formidable generosity, a feeling that is present in all the places mentioned, and which establish and confirm their identity. In embarking on the adventure of the Mondrian, Starck recognizes that he wanted to use the aesthetic and cultural background of Los Angeles as a means of bringing out his conception of society at large.

"I wanted this place to become a sort of oasis of love, friendship, tenderness," he states. "My reflections were dictated by a dual wish for elegance and honesty. Ian Schrager and I dreamed of creating a place full of mystery and adventure that would bring its guests more than ordinary happiness, a feeling closer to jubilation."

The dream has come true. From the moment the visitor crosses the threshold, he is drawn into a contact with the hotel. Entering through the giant door that fronts on the Boulevard and walking into the monumental hall, Stark's obsession for theatrical staging is palpable. A marble table, totally disproportionate in size, seems to point to the three elevators in their glass cage. The table reinterprets the traditional functions of lunch, dinner or simply having a drink. By placing people face to face, it serves to foster contacts and encounters, an idea ever close to the hearts of our two accomplices.

Each one of the 245 rooms offers a breathtaking view of the city. Completely equipped and decorated by Starck, they have been conceived as little apartments, so that each guest can feel as much at home as possible. White sofas, filtered light, heavy curtain and small tables with clean lines – elegance à la Starck. From the original apartment building there remained the kitchens. Each room has one, and you can use it to make yourself a freshly-squeezed orange juice or prepare a cup of tea or coffee or, if you like, to have a whole feast sent up for a meal with friends.

The hotel has several restaurants, bars and boutiques, as well as a terrace offering a magical panorama over Los Angeles. Here in this space open to the sky, Starck and Schrager have amused themselves like a couple of school boys, mixing *Alice in Wonderland* with *Lady Chatterley's Lover.* The Alice side is visible in the immense flower pots with their profusion of flowering plants that seem to break all rules of scale and proportion. But around the swimming pool hovers an ambiance that would not have been out of place in ancient Rome.

Throughout the hotel, aside from original creations by Starck, furniture from around the world (from Paris flea

Only a door separates Sunset Boulevard from the wonderful world of Mondrian.

Opposite page
At the foot of the giant potted ficus plants, a heterogeneous grouping of chairs and beds, of teak or rattan, draped and tasseled, for sitting and lounging, set out in such a way as to encourage quiet conversation, sleep or blissful idleness.

Following pages
The swimming pool and its panoramic views over the city: feet in the water, a drink in hand, and eyes on the far horizon...

The kitchen functions round the clock, from morning breakfast to midnight tapas. Served at an extra-long marble table flanked by chairs and stools of every size and shape.

Starck loves to play with transparency, as here where a glass door opens on a glass cage. The only opaque objects visible are the two curiously-shaped doorknobs.

Opposite page
A bedroom in tones of palest cream, restful and elegant, with candles burning on the bedside table and the dramatic view of Los Angeles beyond the window.

markets or from as far away as Singapore and Brazil) sets a tone of freedom, passage, exchange of ideas.

With the Mondrian, Starck and Schrager pursue their joint experience, going ever further in their philosophy of style, where glamour is mixed with natural feeling, true comfort and a real sense of the "other." Perhaps the key words to sum up their work are: uncomplicated sophistation. □

HOTEL LA PEROUSE

Barto & Barto

Hôtel La Pérouse

Nantes, France

The Hôtel La Pérouse, built in the heart of Nantes by the husband-and-wife team of architects, Bernard and Clotilde Barto. Its smooth white facade catches the eye and disconcerts the viewer who tries to match the windows with the number of floors (or with the surrounding levels.)

"**T**his building was constructed to be here, not elsewhere..." Bernard Barto speaks with a certainty that is comforting. As he explains the construction of the Hôtel La Pérouse in the French city of Nantes, his talk is studded with telling words: compact, monolithic, block, plenitude, sensibility – words as weighty as anchors. Never used by chance.

Situated in the heart of the city, the hotel stands at the edge of an 18th-century quarter. The neighboring buildings, heavy and opulent, were in fact the first constraint. The new building to be created had to find the material quality of this strong and demanding city landscape. Another imperative – to superimpose seven levels in a surrounding height usually (one could almost say culturally) limited to four.

"Architecture is made of constraints. Otherwise, it is art..." One can imagine how the idea was born. A pencil line drawn like a statement of the obvious. Just the right line, to insert the project into the urban tissue of Nantes. To make it exist and breathe in its context. With a rigor that is nearly mystical, to plant the building in its decor. Still, an idea is nothing if you fail to carry it to fruition. Hence, a search for solutions, fighting against doubt, disbelief and the prevailing conformism.

An utterly pared-down look. Here the entrance is brought to life only by the warmth of the wood.

Horizontality of windows. Absence of balconies. No roof – or rather a roof that is no more than the extension of a wall, of the same material as the facade. One can imagine the battles to be fought, the minds to convince. But the line follows its line... "And why this sloping side? Could the hand have slipped?" Let us be reassured – the hand knows its art. It advances without trembling. The slope is merely inspired by a number of the stately homes of this city. To this aesthetic explanation, a practical corollary. The slope creates additional space – never forget, it is a hotel we are building.

An edifice that is smooth, with no asperities, no balconies, no pipes or gutters. Rub out all that is superfluous. What seems simple on paper poses a multitude of concrete problems. For the drainpipes, two walls are built, a structural one, masked by a wall of stone. The water runs down under this "skin." To dissimulate without lying. The absence of balconies is a foregone conclusion – the horizontal effect demands it. There is no trickery, no dressing up. A window is a window, a door a door.

The same on the inside. Make your choice and stick to it. Barto & Barto never forget that this is a hotel. The seven levels to be created impose choices. This dictates the irregular positioning of the windows, a liberty possible in a hotel. In the rooms, the windows may be high or low, so that the guest is confronted directly with the design of the building. As for the furnishings, there is plenty of glass and tile and plexiglass, the rigor of straight lines, the purity of Zen. Typical Barto & Barto.

One cannot imagine this building in any other city. From the outset, it attracted considerable attention. That was to be expected. A project like this does not go unnoticed. The main thing is what remains, what stands the test of time. Heavy, massive, reassuring. Let the winds blow, the stone lives amid stone. A new stone among the old. This is the way cities grow and survive – from this perpetual dialogue of stone. Barto & Barto are not about to stop up their ears. They are like stones that answer one another, terribly alive. □

A side view of the hotel showing the superposed horizontal windows. With their fondness for mural art, Barto & Barto have used this smooth white wall as a pretext for a plastic composition. The window glass reflects fractured images of the world around it.

The dining room would not feel out of place in a monastery. Pure Barto & Barto, it reaches the limits of austerity, but for the warm glow of the wood.

The entrance, with
plain sofas of tubular
steel. The windows as
seen from inside.

Purity of line and transparency of form in bathrooms all of glass or plexiglass.

Opposite page
To the smoothness of the glass is added the texture of mosaic tile.

OMA - Rem Koolhaas

Hotel Furkablick

Furka Pass, Switzerland

The delicate modifications brought by Rem Koolhaas have given the venerable Furkablick Hotel (built in 1890 and enlarged in 1903) a new lease on life.

Opposite page
The bar, with concrete counter, wall of pressed wood shavings, accordion pleated ceiling and aluminum staircase.

The hotel with its two contiguous buildings and a new entrance from the driveway.

In an age of jet planes, high-speed trains and tunnels piercing the heart of the mountains, the once-busy road through the Alpine passes is hardly used nowadays, except by a few nonchalant tourists, black leather jacketed motorcycle enthusiasts and bike champions accomplishing feats of endurance. The inns all along the vertiginous route have gradually fallen into disuse.

The Hotel Furkablick, which stands on the narrow road through the Furka Pass at an altitude of 2,435 meters, in the beautiful canton of Uri (known by crossword puzzle solvers), had been closed for over ten years and seemed doomed to slow decrepitude when Marc Hostettler bought it in 1983. To run such an establishment, which can remain open only for the three summer months each year, can seem a hazardous venture. But Hostettler, who owns an art gallery in Neuchatel, had another idea in mind. His aim was to make Furkablick a center of contemporary art, while continuing to offer lodging to wandering travelers and athletic souls on biking tours testing their skills at the demanding altitude of the pass.

To attract a select group of artists each year during the short season, he had to find a way to restore some of its

On the western facade of the old building, Koolhaas has added a sort of box to serve as an entranceway and fitted out the space around it. Walking into this glass and aluminum structure one feels rather like entering the bellows of an old-fashioned camera.

bygone luster to the hotel that had seen better days. Looking around him, he chose Max Bill to adorn the summit of the pass and the architect Luc Leleu to arrange adjoining building. For the hotel, Hostettler thought of John Hejduk, the legendary guru of Cooper Union, New York's renowned school of architecture

The hotel consists of two buildings, one erected in 1890, with 10 rooms, and the second a square block of 27 rooms added in 1903. It offers still today a fine rustic comfort, Swiss style, with cozy wooden beds and ceramic basins for morning ablutions. Apart from adding a new dining room, the proposed program was singularly vacuous. John Hejduk came for a quick look and... politely declined the offer.

And then, Rem Koolhaas, who was in the neighborhood, stopped in. He was thrilled by the awesome grandeur of the site, and challenged by an unexpected mix of a clientele where meditative poets rubbed shoulders with muscular athletes. The project agreed upon was to preserve the older parts, with their authentic rusticity, and to update the facilities to meet the standards of hygiene and security of a modern hotel. They placed the dining room on the ground floor of the older building, on the side facing the road. The manufacturer of Ebel watches, who had renovated Le Corbusier's Villa Turque, brought his support to the undertaking.

It is said that when Fieldmarshal Rommel visited Malaparte at his home in Capri, the writer told him: "I didn't build the house, I built the landscape." Koolhaas could make the same claim. First he opened up a large vertical window encompassing the two lower levels of the facade facing the valley, in such a way that the landscape would form an integral part of the inside. He added a delicate thin steel terrace with a wooden floor, set slightly apart from the building, as if suspended in space. It is on a level with the dining room and connects to the adjoining platform by a fragile walkway. A thin concrete partition forms a bar both inside and out. The cavity of the metal staircase leading to the kitchens is open on the slope.

The design combines great simplicity with the highest sophistication – the palest of wall coverings, a wooden parquet floor, the smooth concrete of the counter and one wall of pressed wood shavings. The ceiling is covered by perforated insulation plaques, with folded aluminum over the staircase. A 60° arc is left flat – a combination of beauty and efficiency – to allow for a partial opening of the vast window. With the exception of this one detail, and of a glass and

From the lounge, the gaze flows uninterrupted through the bar, out the broad window, onto the deck and into the mountainous landscape beyond.

View of the terrace and the concrete counter that passes through the window.

Over the staircase, the accordion pleated aluminum ceiling is interrupted by a smooth 60° arc that makes it possible to open the window.

The fine metal structure of the bridge cum walkway seems suspended in space.

metal box that form an entrance chamber, everything is remarkably understated. The concept plays essentially on the contrast of sensations: the quiet comfort of the room and the breathtaking grandeur of the landscape. Koolhaas's design is supremely in tune with the site.

As for the artwork, Hostettler has avoided making it either a spectacle – except for some ephemeral appearances – or, as many others have not managed to avoid, a decoration. Visitors exploring the surroundings will come upon the works of art sprinkled in the midst of nature: the four parallelepipeds posed by Max Bill at the very top of the pass, where one stops to take in the panorama, and which passing picnickers are free to use; the sculpture by Kirkenby, a discreet brick creation at the summit; after that you have to stroll along trails, thick with grass and strewn with rocks, to discover a Fibonaci-esque stele by Mario Merz, or one of the sayings by Jenny Holzer scattered here and there. For guests too lazy to go exploring, Hostettler has assembled these truisms on a table mat, though he is careful not to mention the fact. To cite one taken at random: "Killing is inevitable, but it's nothing to be proud of." □

The concrete assemblage by Max Bill is put to good use by passers by.

At the very top of the pass, the brick sculpture by Kirkenby stands like a marker or a signpost.

Opposite page
On a hallway window, the artist Marc Luyten has left his mark, so discreet as to be nearly imperceptible.

Following pages
General view of the hotel in its setting of Alpine mists.

(le miroir)

José Paulo dos Santos

Pousada de Nossa Senhora da Asunção

Arraiolos, Portugal

The former Convent dos Lóios, dating from the 16th century, ceased to be a religious building in 1834, and is now a hotel for holidaymakers in Northern Portugal. Restored and rehabilitated, it is today extended by a new wing and its esplanade.

Opposite page
An immaculate facade gives onto the large patio. José dos Santos has remodeled the door and window frames in blond wood.

Following pages
A patio, olive trees, a large water basin and some traditional terra cotta jars: an homage to the simplicity of the monastic life. In the background, in the new wing, a restaurant with an entire wall of glass opens on the other side toward the swimming pool.

Every site speaks with its own voice. To hear what these places are saying and feel what they bring us from the past – this is a virtue in which some architects seem to be sadly lacking. This need to listen, far from restricting creativity, often proves to bring the needed responses to the questions raised by a project. When the architect José Paulo dos Santos undertook to remodel a former convent into a luxury hotel, he understood immediately that the original function of this monumental building would guide all his endeavor.

Peace and serenity. In no way would he do anything to alter these essential qualities dictated by the religious heritage of the building. On the contrary, his challenge was to transform the convent in accordance with clearly-defined criteria of hotel comfort, without betraying the contemplative spirit of the place. In short, he had to succeed in two things at once: to make proper use of the environment (which is both simple and sophisticated) and to create an easy-to-decipher dialogue between the sometimes austere existing architecture and all the functional items – furniture and facilities – that had to be introduced.

The exceptional site of Southern Portugal was naturally decisive in the conception of the project. A bright blue sky and a mountain covered with olive groves – in this clear-cut,

 Pousada de Nossa Senhora da Asunção, Arraiolos, Portugal

In the portion of the vast space destined to become the dining room, the architect had to break up the monumental height, in order to attenuate the austerity and create an smaller, more intimate area.

The stark lines of the furniture express a striving for inner peace, under the vaulted ceiling, completely restored. Would anyone really suspect that this is a bar?

In the lounge the deep sofas and armchairs of blue and white stand in quiet simplicity on a floor covered with hemp matting.

Opposite page
The walls of azulejo tile, which date from the 18th century and depict the lives of the saints, illuminate the former chapel of the convent.

The patio seen from the roof, bounded by the new wing.

The swimming pool, extended by the esplanade and the gardens. For a hint of traditional blue, the architect dos Santos and his decorator Cristina Guedes have included delicate touches of the azulejo color in pillars and tapestries, armchairs and chair covers, or the flower pattern of a tablecloth...

Opposite page
The cloister with the rooms leading off it. Like cloisters of old, it is a call to contemplation and a search for inner peace.

unembellished setting, the whiteness of the convent appears as a haven of serenity. The new wing frankly proclaims its kinship with the older part. It is like a new stone added to an old edifice, which wants to blend in with the original structure while at the same time fulfilling the new mission given to it, in this case, adding the complementary facilities of hotel accommodation.

In accordance with the wishes of those who initiated the project, the convent therefore retains its total sobriety, both in structure and in the materials used. It is completely reorganized, with three levels, each playing a distinct role. The lowest level, deeply cut into the earth, holds all the utilities and services necessary for the daily functioning of a hotel. Above this are the public areas, centered around three vital organs – the cloisters, the patio and the esplanade. In the patio, a pool prefigures the sumptuous swimming pool that has been built intentionally out of the way, in the extension of the new wing.

The upper floor houses the 30 bedrooms and two suites, spread over the old wing and the new.

The materials are as sober as the site. Stucco, stone, marble and wood follow the monastic tradition. Granite and green schist cover most of the floors on the public level. In the new part, oak parquet floors add a warm touch to rooms and hallways. Bathrooms use a local marble, while beds, tables and chairs are of oak or cherrywood.

In short, if the entire project reveals a desire to blend into a predominant historical reality, the modesty of the approach should not make us overlook the remarkable synthesis – by which a place dedicated to prayer has been successfully transformed into an incomparable holiday site. All that remains of the former severity is a gentle, soothing sobriety. The spare lines of the new building and the quality of the materials used, enhanced by the shimmering presence of the water, combine to enfold the traveler in a feeling of plenitude, to bestow on all visitors the blessings of peaceful contentment. □

A "cell" of monastic simplicity in the new wing, its only decoration the pattern of the slatted headboards against the black background. The floor and side tables are of oak.

Opposite page
In the lobby, the monumental fireplace attracts the eye: its impressive size befits this vast convent cum hotel.

The bathrooms are decorated with a local marble.

o, non popolo antico,
a:
ti,
odini,
sporchi,
li zii bigotti,
gia libera, un bordello!
nilioni di porci
illesi palazzotti,
mai come chiese.
I non esisti,
osciente sei incoscient
on puoi pensare
colpa di ogni male.
mare, libera il mondo.

PASOLINI

Antonio Presti

Atelier sul mare

Castel di Tusa, Sicily, Italy

On a private terrace looking out over the Bay of Castel di Tusa, perhaps some visitors will have a thought for the poor fishermen of Visconti's *La terra trema*...

Opposite page
... Others, their curiosity aroused by these lines cited in the bathroom of Antonio Presti's room, may want to read the works of Pasolini and reflect on *il cinema italiano.*

Although it is situated on one of the most beautiful bays in Sicily, between Messina and Palermo, the growing reputation of the hotel Atelier sul Mare is not due to its site, but rather to the fact that 14 of its 40 rooms are designed by artists of international fame.

To sum up the intention of the owner, Antonio Presti, one need only listen to the Japanese artist Nagasawa, whose room *Mistero per la luna* presents itself as a synthesis of the most refined Japanese and Western influences. "I imagine the traveler arriving at the Atelier, getting his key at the desk and finding himself a few minutes later in his room on the other side of a closed door. From that moment on, he is not in a hotel bedroom but in a museum space of his own, within which he will live a unique experience. For an hour or two days or a week he will live in perfect osmosis with a work of art conceived just for him, built to his dimensions..."

Antonio Presti has always had the greatest enthusiasm for all that touches the world of art. But for many years his artistic pursuits remained secondary to his activity as a hotelier. The shock of his father's death in 1984 marked the beginning of a new phase in his life, when these two worlds

Red on blue, a geometric vision by Mauro Staccioli (1993)

Opposite page
The "hall of mirrors," part of the *Stanza del Profeta,* the room in homage to Pier Paolo Pasolini (1995).

began their strange coexistence. "When my father died," says Presti, "I imagined a stone shaken loose from the mountain that the movement of its fall carries to the sea. It was why I asked the sculptor Pietro Consagra to build a work at the mouth of the Tusa." This was the first step of an uncommon adventure that led him to erect seven sculptures on this portion of the Sicilian coast and eventually caused him some problems with the law for having failed to get proper authorization in advance.

When he emerged victorious from his judicial battles, Presti grew bolder and decided to let art penetrate his hotel by entrusting several of the rooms to artists, at first Sicilian artists for the most part. They were given carte blanche, Presti's only intervention being to talk with them at length and imbue himself with their projects. The result lived up to the dreams of this hotel owner who is also a patron of the arts. Whether it be the inverted pyramid enthroned in the middle of the room by Mauro Staccioli or the nest-shaped bed imagined by Paolo Icaro, *Il nido,* the various works

cannot fail to provoke reflections in the mind of a visitor seeking new sensations. Presti is not the only one enthralled by his own unusual experiment. Reservation requests for these museumlike spaces have steadily risen in relation to those for the ordinary rooms.

Those who want to carry things to an extreme can choose the room designed by Fabrizio Plessi, a vast space whose walls are covered by doors, above which a row of television screens, facing the bed, show an endlessly repeated image of the sea. The sceptical soul may shout impostor or object that if you put in a window in place of the doors, you'd have a real view of the sea. Yet despite this, Plessi's *Stanza del mare negato* is among the rooms most in demand.

Presti has even asked filmmakers like Raoul Ruiz to take part in the experience. He went so far as to meet with Renato Curcio, a former member of the Red Brigades conditionally out of prison, who was delighted with his proposal and agreed to work with the artist Agostino Ferrari on the history of writing. Their joint project, based on prison graffiti, is now visible on the walls and ceiling of a room.

Wanting a direct role in his own project, Presti reserved the design of one room for himself, dedicated to the filmmaker Pier Paolo Pasolini. An inscription in the bathroom reminds the cinema fan that "we are what we excrete," a comment that makes Antonio Presti smile. □

The room called "The Nest" by Paolo Icaro (1990-91): ever wondered what it feels like to sleep inside an egg?

Opposite page
The birth of writing, as inspired by prison graffiti. The room by Renato Curcio, with Agostino Ferrari and Gianni Ruggeri is named *Sogni tra segni* (1994).

One room reduced to a bed, a view of the sea and the artist's work on the walls. By Piero Dorazio and Graziano Marini: untitled (1996). Another draws the gaze upward as if in a dream landscape. This one is by filmmaker Raoul Ruiz and is called *La Torre di Sigismondo* (1993), a reference to one of his recent films, *Turris eburnea,* part of which was shot in Castel di Tusa in 1994.

Entitled *Energia* by Maurizio Machetti (1992). The bright red fairly pulsates with violence and passion.

Following pages
A bed perched on a pedestal like an altar in the center of a chapel: in *La stanza della terra e del fuoco* by Luigi Mainolfi (1996) all the surfaces are completely covered with tile and adorned with wire sculptures that form a chair and ceiling fixture.

The bathroom by Renato Curcio has a timeless look as if emerging from some primeval grotto.

Of all the non-conformist rooms in this non-conformist establishment, this one is certainly the most iconoclastic (or outrageous?) of all. Called *Stanza del mare negato,* it is totally enclosed by doors, with the sea visible only on a row of television screens, by Fabrizio Plessi (1992).

The room of the Prophet, decorated with Arabic calligraphy and dedicated to filmmaker/poet Pasolini. The apartment is the work of Dario Belleza, Adele Cambria, Gianni Ruggeri and Antonio Presti himself, with the collaboration of Laura Betti (1995).

Biographies

Barto & Barto

BARTO Bernard and Clotilde

Artists born in Nantes, respectively in 1937 and 1948.
Bernard Barto graduated from the painting section of the Ecole des Beaux-Arts in Nantes in 1959. Clotilde has a degree in psychopathology (1980). As a couple they have worked on a great many buildings (designing color schemes and providing murals, sculptures and frescoes. Worked with Jean Nouvel on Cultural Centers of Saint-Herblain and Melun-Sénart.

Works: In Nantes, posters and catalogues for the Decorative Arts Museum (1972-1977), Chézine house (1977), Audi-VW garage (1988), hotel in downtown Nantes (1989-1993).

BRANSON COATES ARCHITECTURE LTD

BRANSON doug

Born in Great Britain in 1951.
Graduated from the Architectural Association School of Architecture (1975).
Works at J.F.N. in New York, Norman Westwater. Associated architect DEGW in London (1976-1978).
Partnership with Nigel Coates since 1985.
Taught at AA (1975-1977) and at Canterbury College of Art (1976).

COATES Nigel

Born in 1949 in Malvern, Great Britain.
Graduated from Architectural Association School of Architecture, London, 1974.
Founded his agency with Doug Branson in London in 1985.
Has taught since 1995 at the Royal College of Art, London.
Awarded Japan Inter-Design Prize (1990).

Major Works: restaurant Metropole (1985) and café Bongo (1986) in Tokyo, Jasper Conran shops in London (1986), Dublin (1987) and Tokyo (1989), hotel Otaru Marittimo in Otaru, Japan (1989), Jigsaw fashion shops in London, Tokyo, Dublin and Manchester (since 1988), Nishi Azabu Building, called "The Wall" in Tokyo (1990), night club Taxim in Istanbul (1991), Art Gallery Silo in Tokyo (1993), Bargo bar in Glasgow (1996), National Center for Popular Music in Sheffield (1996-98).
Design : vases for Simon Moore (1996), Allessi (1990) ; aluminum objects for 100% Design (1995) ; furniture for Partner and Co (1997), Poltronova, Arredaesse, Bros's, SCP...

BURKHALTER + SUMI

BURKHALTER Marianne

Swiss architect.
From 1970 to 1984, worked for different agencies : Superstudio in Florence (1969-1972), Studio Works, New York (1970-1976), Studio Works, Los Angeles (1977-1978).
In partnership with Christian Sumi in 1984, opened an agency in Zürich.
Visiting professor at Southern Institute of Architecture, Los Angeles, in 1987.

SUMI Christian

Born in Biel, Switzerland, in 1950.
Graduated from ETH, Zürich (1977).
Visiting professor at Geneva Architectural School (1990-1991) and Harvard (1994).

Major Works of the agency:
in Switzerland, Pircher house in Eglisau and Brunner house in Langnau (1984-1986), renovation of old buildings in Kaiserstuhl (1988-1990), kindergarten in Lustenau (1992-1994), hotel Zürichberg in Zürich (1993-1995), apartment buildings in Laufenburg (1994-1995), hotel Dorinth in Weimar, Germany (1996-1997).

DÖRING Wolfgang

Born in Berlin in 1934.
Studied at the Technische Hochschule in Munich, then in Darmstadt.
In 1964 opened his agency in Düsseldorf.
In 1970 published Perspektiven einer Architektur.
Has taught at the Technische Hochschule in Aachen since 1973.

Works: Wabbel residence in Düsseldorf, (1965), hotel and restaurant Rolandsburg (1980-1984), Döring apartment in Bonn (1983-1984).

DORNER Marie-Christine

Born in Strasbourg in 1960.
Graduated from Nissim-de-Camondo School, Paris (1984).
Worked for Jean-Michel Wilmotte, then lived in Japan for a year (1986), where she was in contact avec the group Idee, who put out her first collection of light fixtures, shown at the Axis Gallery.
In 1987 founded her agency of interior design and architecture in Paris.
Taught at the Ecole supérieure d'art and de design in Reims (1991-1995).
Grand Prize for Creation of the city of Paris (1995).

Works: Design objects: furniture for Scarabat, Spain (1988), Artelano and Opaque diffusion (1989), designed presidential tribune for the July 14th (Bastille Day) parade (1990).
Architecture : hotel La Villa, Saint-Germain-des-Prés, offices of the French Association of Artistic Action (avec Roche, DVS & Co, 1995).

ITO Toyo

Born in Seoul in 1941.
Graduated from the University of Tokyo (1965).
Worked at the agency Kiyonori Kikutake until 1969.
Founded his agency in 1971, which took the name of Toyo Ito Architect & Associates in 1979.

Major projects: U-House (1976) and Hotel D (1977) in Nagano, PMT House in Nagoya (1978), residence Silver Hut in Tokyo (1984), Tower of the Winds in Yokohama, Kanagawa (1986), kindergartens in Eckenheim and Frankfurt (1988-1991), apartment building Pao 2 for Tokyo Nomad Woman in Bruxelles (1989), municipal museum of Yatsushiro, Kumamoto (1989-1991), home for the aged (1992-1994) and firehouse (1992-1995) of Yatsushiro, Kyushu island, Shimasuwa Museum Lake Suwa, Shimasuwa-machi, Nagano (1990-1993).

NALBACH + NALBACH

NALBACH Johanne

Born in Linz, Austria, in 1943.
Graduated from the Technische Hochschule of Vienna (1969).
Opened an agency with Gernot Nalbach in Berlin in 1975.
Assistant professor since 1996 at Kansas State University, Lawrence, Kansas.

NALBACH Gernot

Born in 1942 in Vienne.
Graduated from the Technische Hochschule in Vienna (1968).
Since 1975, visiting professor in Brasilia, Moscow, Amsterdam, Utrecht.

Major Works of the agency: in Berlin, interior design of the Grand Hotel Esplanade and the Art'otel (1990), renovation and scenography of Münster Museum (1992), hotel in Nakenstorf near Wismar (1993), concert hall for Fine Arts School in Berlin (1995), as well as many subsidized housing projects and residences in Berlin and Leipzig.

NOUVEL Jean

Born in Fumel in 1945.
Graduated DPLG (1972).
Co-founder of French architectural movement "Mars 1976". Co-founder of the Syndicat de l'Architecture and organizer of the consultation Quartier des Halles (1979). founder and art director of the Biennale d'Architecture (1980).
Grand Prix in Architecture, won Equerre d'argent for the Institute of the Arab World and Creator of the Year at the Paris Furniture Show (1987). Prize of Architectural Record for the hotel Saint-James(1990). Equerre d'argent for the Opera house of Lyon (1993).
Honorary member of the AIA Chicago (1993) and RIBA (1995).

Major Works: renovation of the Theater of Belfort (1984), Luzard gymnasium in Marne-la-Vallée and La Coupole cultural center in Combs-la-Ville (1986), Institute of the Arab World in Paris (1987), housing units Némausus in Nîmes (1988), Onyx cultural center in Saint-Herblain (with Myrto Vitart), hotel Amat Bordeaux in Bouliac, INIST documentation center of CNRS in Nancy (1989), Cartier building in Villeret, Switzerland (1992), Hotel des Thermes in Daw, Pierre and Vacances housing units at Cap d'Ail (1992), Opera House in Lyon, Congress Center in Tours, subsidized housing in Bezons (1993), Cartier Foundation in Paris, Euralille Center, Galeries Lafayette complex and shops in Berlin (1994-1996).
In progress: cultural and congress center in Lucerne, Switzerland, judicial complex in Nantes, Cognacq-Jay Foundation in Rueil-Malmaison, central office of Interunfall in Bregenz, Austria.

OBLIERS Dirk

Born in Bochum, Germany, in 1949.
Graduated from the University of Essen/Folkwang School(1974) in visual communications and design.
In 1989, created his agency of hotel design and scenography, based at the castle of Döhlau, Germany.

OMA - REM KOOLHAAS

KOOLHAAS Rem

Born in Rotterdam in 1944.
Journalist and writer of filmscripts.
Studied at the Architectural Association of London (1968-1972). In 1972 won a scholarship to the United States.
Worked with Oswald-Mathias Ungers at Cornell University (1972-1973), then with Peter Eisenman, at the Institute for Architecture and Urban Studies, New York.
In London in 1975 founded Oma, Office for Metropolitan Architecture with architects Elia and Zoé Zenghelis and Madelon Vriesendorp.
In 1978, published Delirious New York, and in 1979 designed a retrospective of New York architect, Wallace Harrison entitled Beyond good or bad, for the IAUS.
In 1980 opened an agency in Rotterdam.
Visiting fellow at IAUS until 1979. Also taught at Columbia University, UCLA and the Architectural Association. Since 1990, professor at Harvard.

Works: in The Netherlands, The Hague, National Dance Theater (1987), Rotterdam bus station (1987), Patiovilla (1988), Kunsthal Rotterdam (1991) ; Brink buildings in Gröningen (1988), RWA workshops in Amersfoort (1990), shops and offices Bysantium in Amsterdam (1991), Educatorium of University of Utrecht (1997) ; in France, villa Dall'Ava in Saint-Cloud (1991), Euralille and Lille-Grand-Palais, villa de Bordeaux (1998) ; in Switzerland, hotel Furkablick at Furka Pass (1990) and in Japan, Nexus complex in Fukuoka (1991).
In progress: University Museum in Seoul, Droits de l'Homme Building in Geneva, commercial zone in Utrecht, Dutch Embassy in Berlin, Hyperbuilding in Bangkok.

PUTMAN Andrée

Born in Paris in 1925.
Art director for Créateurs et Industriels, then for Mafia, design and communication agency founded by

Denise Fayolle and Maimé Arnodin.
In 1978, founded Ecart, agency of architecture, interior architecture and design, and Ecart International, distributor of furniture and design objects, producing and distributing emblematic objects of the 20th century (Black Board rug by Eileen Gray, metal chair by Mallet-Stevens, lamp by Mariano Fortuny...).
National Grand Prize for industrial design, 1995.

Works
Architecture : shop design for Thierry Mugler (1978), Hémisphères (with J.-F. Bodin, 1981), Yves Saint-Laurent in San Francisco (1982), Azzedine Alaïa (1985), Ebel in London, Paris and New York (1986-1988), Carita (1988), Balenciaga (1989), scenography of Ecart showroom (with Robert Wilson, 1985), remodeling of offices for Karl Lagerfeld (1982), the Ministry of Culture (1984) ; hotels: Morgan's in New York, Wasserturm in Cologne (1987), Contemporary Art Museum, Bordeaux (1984), Fine Arts Museum, Rouen (1985-1992), re-design of Concorde (1992-1993)...
Design objects: furniture for Culture Ministry (1984), Finance Ministry (1987), Rouen Fine Arts Museum (1992), Putman line for Les Trois Suisses...

ROSSI Aldo
Born in Milan in 1931, died in 1997.
Graduated from the Milan Politecnico in 1959.
From 1955 to 1964 worked for the magazine Casabella Continuita.
In 1966 published L'architettura della citta.
Taught at University of Palermo (1970), Politecnico of Milan (1972/73), Polytechnic of Zürich, as well as at Yale, Harvard, and the Institute for Architecture in New York.
Pritzker Prize in 1990.

Major Works: housing in Gallaratese quarter in Milan (1973), cemetery San Cataldo, with Gianni Braghieri, in Modena (1971), Théâtre du Monde, Venice (1979), Rauchstrasse apartments in Berlin (1983), residential buildings for the show Internationale Bauausstellung in Berlin (1984-87), Centro Torri in Parma (1985-88), Architecture School for the University of Miami (1986), theater Toronto Lighthouse, with Morris Adjimi, in Toronto (1988), hotel Il Palazzo in Fukuoka, Japan (1989).

DOS SANTOS Jose Paulo
Studied in Canterbury (1975-1978),then at Royal College of Arts, London (1979-1981).
Member of the group "9H".
Since 1984, based in Porto, Portugal.

Works: in Porto, restoration of Turismo do Lusa (1985-1987), Palace Hotel da Curia (1987-1988), hotel do Buçaco (1987-1992).

STARCK Philippe
Born in Paris in 1949.
Ecole Nissim-de-Camondo, Paris.
Created Starck Product in 1979.
Has taught at Domus Academy in Milan and l'Ecole nationale des arts décoratifs in Paris.
National Grand Prize for industriel design in France (1988).

Major Works
Interior architecture: in Paris, La Main Bleue (1976), Les Bains Douches (1978), Café Costes (1984), restaurant Manin and Café Mystique in Tokyo (1986), hotels Royalton and Paramount in New York (1988 and 1990), restaurants Teatriz in Madrid (1990), Peninsula in Hong Kong (1994), Theatron in Mexico (1995), Asia de Cuba in New York (1997).
Architecture: cutlery factory Laguiole in France (1988), office buildings Nani Nani and Asahi in Tokyo (1989), Ecole nationale des arts décoratifs, Paris (1995), waste disposal plant in Paris/Vitry (to be completed in 2004).
Design : furniture for Elysée Palace,numerous designs for furniture and objects distributed in France, Italy, Spain, Japan, Switzerland and Germany.
Industriel design: Bénéteau boats, Daum vases, Aprilia scooter, Fluocaril toothbrush, Mikli eyeglasss, Decaux street equipment, etc...

UCHIDA Shigeru
Born in Yokohama, Japan, in 1943.
Graduated from Kuwasawa Design School, Tokyo (1966).
In 1970 created his agency.
Lecturer at Kuwasawa School (1973-) and University of art and design, Tokyo (1974-1978).
In 1981 founded Studio 80, with Toru Nishioka.
Japan Interior Designers Association Award (1981), Mainichi prize (1987), special prize for best shop design of the year (1990), Grand Prize Shokankyo (1990).
Lectured at American Universities (Columbia, Parsons School of Design in 1986), Domus Academy (1992) and Politecnico of Milan (1995), and Dutch Center of Utrecht (1996).

Major Works
Design : Free-Form-Chair (1969), September chairs (1977), Nirvana (1981), Ny Chair II (1986), lamp Tenderly (1985), clocks Dear Morris and Dear Vera (1989)...
Architecture : in Tokyo, stores Seibu (1975-1980) and Tobu (1992), shops Issey Miyake (1976-1982) and Yohji Yamamoto (1983-1986), manicure parlor Longleage in Hiroo (1997), bar Le Club in Roppongi (1986), restaurants Yuzutei in Nishiazabu (1986) and La Ranarita in Azumabashi (1991) ; hôtels Il Palazzo in Fukuoka (1989) and Lobby in Kyoto (1994) ; tea houses Ji-An, Gyo-an & So-An (1993), Fashion Museum of the city of Kobé (1997).

DE VOS Dorine
Born in Djakarta in 1948.
Since 1979, has worked both as a graphist/illustrator (book covers and illustrations, posters, writing paper, brochures, etc) and a decorator.
Chief decorator for the films Luba by Alegandro Agresti (1989) and Zondagsjongen by Pieter Verhoeff (1991). Also designs sets for television (1994-1997).

Works: Schlemmer's café/tobacconist's in The Hague (1984) ; in Rotterdam, cafés restaurants Zochers (1986), Loos and Floor (1987), hotel New York (with Daan vd Have and Hans Loos, 1993), studio Zeeland (1998).

Bibliography

General bibliography
FITOUSSI Brigitte, *Hôtels*, Publications du Moniteur, 1992.
GEN Takeshi Saito, *American Hotels and their Restaurants*, Shotenkenchiku, Tokyo.

Monographs
BERTONI Franco, *Philippe Starck, l'architecture*, Pierre Mardaga éditeur, Liège, 1994.
BOISSIÈRE Olivier, *Jean Nouvel*, Terrail.
FAWCET Anthony, *New British Interiors : Nigel Coates – Zaha Hadid,* Art Random, Tokyo, 1991.
GOULET Patrice, *Jean Nouvel*, Editions du Regard/Institut Français d'Architecture, Paris, 1994.
LUCAN Jacques, *OMA-Rem Koolhaas*, Electa/Moniteur, 1990.
MORRIS Adjimi, *Aldo Rossi : Architecture 1981-1991*, New York, 1991.
OMA/Rem KOOLHAAS and MAU Bruce, *S, M, L, XL*, 010 Publishers/The Monacelli Press, New York, 1995. Benedikt Taschen, Cologne, 1997.
POYNOR Rick, *Nigel Coates : The City in Motion*, Fourth Estate, London, 1989.
ROULET Sophie & SOULIÉ Sophie, *Toyo Ito*, Ed. du Moniteur, Paris, 1991.
TASMA-ANARGYROS Sophie, *Andrée Putman*, Norma, Paris, 1997.
Aldo Rossi : Opera Completa 1957-1996, par Alberto Ferlenga, 3 volumes, Electa, Milan, 1996.
Jean Nouvel, El Croquis n°65/66, Barcelone, 1994. Et aussi, El Croquis " Worldsmundos " (I), n°88/89, Barcelona, 1998.
Starck, Benedikt Taschen, Cologne, 1997.
Toyo Ito, El Croquis n°71, Barcelona, 1995.

Hotel details

SORAT ART'OTEL BERLIN
Joachimstalerstrasse 29 - D-10179 Berlin Charlottenburg
Tel. : +49 (0)30 88 44 70 - Fax : +49 (0)30 88 44 77 00

LA VILLA
29, rue Jacob - F-75006 Paris
Tel. : +33 (0)1 43 26 60 00 - Fax : +33 (0)1 46 34 63 63

HOTEL IM WASSERTURM
Kaygasse 2 - D-50676 Köln
Tel. : +49 (0)2 21 200 80 - Fax : +49 (0)221 200 8888

HOTEL IL PALAZZO
3-13-1, Haruyoshi, Chuo-ku, Fukuoka 810 - Japon
Tel. : +81 (0)92 716 3333 - Fax : +81 (0)92 724 3330

PFLAUMS POSTHOTEL PEGNITZ
Nürnbergerstr. 12-16 - D-91257 Pegnitz
Tel. : +49 (0)9241 7250 - Fax : +49 (0)9241 80404

MONDRIAN
8440 Sunset Boulevard - Los Angeles, CA 90069, USA
Tel. : +1 (213) 650 8999 - Fax : +1 (213) 650 5215

HÔTEL RESTAURANT SAINT-JAMES
3, place Camille Hostein - F-33270 Bouliac
Tel. : +33 (0)5 57 97 06 00 - Fax : +33 (0)5 56 20 92 58

DER TEUFELHOF
Leonhardsgraben 47-49 - CH-4051 Basel
Tel. : +41 (0)61 261 10 10 - Fax : +41 (0)61 261 10 04

DOM BUSINESS HOTEL
Rennbahnstrsse 2 - D-40629 Düsseldorf
Tel. : +49 (0)211 61 00 90 - Fax : +49 (0)211 61 00 943

HOTEL POLUINYA
815 Kiyosato Shari-gun, Hokkaido - 099-4401, Japon
Tel. : +81 1522 5 3800 - Fax : +81 1522 5 3944

HOTEL NEW YORK
Koninginnenhoofd 1 - NL-3072 AD Rotterdam
Tel. : +31 (0)10 4390500 - Fax : +31 (0)10 4842701

HOTEL ZÜRICHBERG
Orellistr. 21 - CH-8044 Zürich
Tel. : +41 (0)1 268 35 35 - Fax : +41 (0)1 268 35 45

POUSADA DE NOSSA SENHORA DA ASUNÇÃO
Convento dos Lóios - 7040 Arraiolos, Portugal
Tel : +351 66 41 93 40/65/70/85 - Fax : +351 66 41 92 80

HOTEL FURKABLICK
Furka Pass - CH-6491 Realp
Tel. : +41 41 887 07 17 - Fax : +41 41 887 12 44

HÔTEL LA PÉROUSE
3, allée Duquesne - F-44000 Nantes
Tel. +33 (0)2 40 89 75 00 - Fax : +33 (0)2 40 89 76 00

ROYALTON
44 West 44 Street - New York City, NY 10036, USA
Tel. : +1 (212) 869 4400 - Fax : +1 (212) 869 8965

MORGANS
237 Madison Avenue - New York City, NY 10016, USA
Tel. : +1 212 686 0300 - Fax : +1 212 779 8352

ATELIER SUL MARE
Via Cesare Battisti, 4 - I-98070 Castel di Tusa (ME)
Tel. : +39 0921-334295 - Fax : +39 0921-334283

Photo credits

Front cover and pages 56 to 65: photos Dirk Obliers
Pages 2, 134 to 145: José Paulo dos Santos archives
Pages 6, 8 to 15, 30 to 39, 40 to 47, 48 to 55, 146 to 157: photos Deidi von Schaewen
Pages 16 to 23: Sorat Art'otel archives
Pages 24 to 29: Aldo Rossi archives
Pages 66 to 73: photos Tomio Ohashi and Naoya Hatakeyama
Pages 74 to 79: photos Rinie Bleeker
Pages 80 to 87, 116 to 123: photos Philippe Ruault
Pages 88 to 93: photos Tomas Riehle
Pages 94 to 101: Teufelhof Hotel archives
Pages 102 to 107: photos Heinrich Helfenstein
Page 103: photo Seiler
Pages 108 to 115, back cover: Ian Schrager Hotels and DKA New York archives
Pages 124 to 133: photos Henriette Denis/AD.OB Design

Printed in Italy